THE MONEY NERVE

THE MONEY NERVE

Navigating the Emotions of Money

Robert Wm Wheeler, CPA

BALBOA.
PRESS
A DIVISION OF HAY HOUSE

Balboa Press books may be ordered through booksellers or by contacting:

Balboa Press
A Division of Hay House
1663 Liberty Drive
Bloomington, IN 47403
www.balboapress.com
1-877-407-4847

Because of the dynamic nature of the Internet, any web addresses or links contained in this book may have changed since publication and may no longer be valid. The views expressed in this work are solely those of the author and do not necessarily reflect the views of the publisher, and the publisher hereby disclaims any responsibility for them.

The author of this book does not dispense medical advice or prescribe the use of any technique as a form of treatment for physical, emotional, or medical problems without the advice of a physician, either directly or indirectly. The intent of the author is only to offer information of a general nature to help you in your quest for emotional and spiritual well-being. In the event you use any of the information in this book for yourself, which is your constitutional right, the author and the publisher assume no responsibility for your actions.

Printed in the United States of America

ISBN: 978-1-4525-6940-6 (sc)
ISBN: 978-1-4525-6942-0 (hc)
ISBN: 978-1-4525-6941-3 (e)

Library of Congress Control Number: 2013903585

Balboa Press rev. date: 04/03/2013

For those who helped me on my path.

The journey continues.

"The real measure of your wealth is how much you'd be worth if you lost all your money."

—Unknown

Contents

Acknowledgments

PUTTING LIFE'S LESSONS INTO PLAIN TEXT IS daunting. I could not have summoned the courage or energy to put forth these ideas without the direct help of Sheldon Anderson. Thank you for challenging me and helping me articulate my position. Thanks to Laurie Davis for marketing advice and Lauren Adams for transcription.

Lori Gudmundson and Lisa Cornwell at Creative Vision Arts kept me focused, organized, and always on the hunt for vivid examples. Thanks to them for their insights and editorial skills.

I am forever grateful for my family, friends, clients, and staff—including Rachel Haimowitz, Deborah Star, Ann Bradney, and Nick Naton, Esq. I am indebted to the organizations that have shaped my perspectives and grounded me, especially Beyond War, the Foundation for Global Community, the Hoffman Institute, and Radical Aliveness Core Energetics. Many heartfelt thanks.

Introduction

Your Money and Your Life

WOULDN'T IT BE NICE TO WORRY LESS about money and focus more on financial freedom? A healthy relationship with money is freedom. It's time to become aware of your personal decision-making process in order to create the new financial you.

How emotions underpin our relationship with money (and how that relationship, in turn, affects all aspects of our lives) is the basis of this book. Each of us has a "Money Nerve," and this book will help you see how your Money Nerve affects your financial decision making.

Reconciling your relationship with money allows you to make wiser choices throughout your life. While you reconcile your relationship with money, you may also discover unexpected benefits in other aspects of your life.

Inherited Responses to Money

Growing up, my grandparents always gave my siblings and me money. They filled our piggy banks and bought us new fishing poles. They even bought each of us grandchildren a car when we turned sixteen. We didn't complain. In essence, they were saying, "Pick us as your favorite grandparents."

When I was a young adult and my grandparents needed some help around the house, I spent a weekend in their yard fixing things up. At the end of the weekend, my grandfather tried to give me a hundred bucks, which I politely refused. My grandparents were very confused and hurt. They could not comprehend that I simply wanted to spend time with them because I loved them.

It wasn't until recently that I realized what my grandparents were really trying to say. My grandparents were really saying, "We don't feel worthy of your love, but if we give you lots of money, will you pretend to love us?" I was totally taken aback and saddened by that thought.

What I came to understand is that my grandmother grew up feeling insecure and unworthy of attention. The only way she could convince people to love her was through bribery, she thought. She taught my mother the same lesson, which not surprisingly trickled down to my siblings and me. I still have the occasional impulse to splurge or use money to solve a problem. Now, though, I understand my emotional response to money and am able to make more conscious choices.

Emotions and Money

Some people say they don't have any emotions about money. And then they start talking about money … and the floodgates open. I developed the Money Nerve idea by working as an accountant, financial advisor, and business consultant for over twenty-five years. I am thankful to the many people and businesses that I've helped who have, in turn, helped me.

I have spent years sitting across the table from my clients—often feeling more like a therapist than an accountant. What I have realized is that many people have money issues, and because they think they are supposed to know how to handle them, they are ashamed to ask for help. I see business owners, other CPAs, lawyers, therapists, doctors, and others in major financial crises.

I am no longer surprised when clients come in, start talking, and break down crying. There is a lot of fear and shame surrounding money. We need to start admitting without shame or embarrassment that we may not have been taught how to handle money (or that we may not know all the answers). We need to bring our money issues out in the open and start changing our belief system about money.

Many people are in denial because they don't want to deal with their financial situation. I had a conversation with a client that went something like this:

Client: I was more upset about coming to see you today than I was about finding out whether or not I had terminal cancer yesterday.

Me: Your priorities are messed up. It's just money.

Client: I didn't want to come to you. I almost canceled. Now I'm glad I'm here—you always make me feel better. I know you're always going to help me and hold my hand. I'm not sure what I was afraid of.

Me: This is only about money. Do you hear what you're saying?

Client: I know, I know.

Huge companies like Fannie May, Freddie Mac, or Lehman Brothers were built on the illusion of wealth. When the time came to pay up, however, their house of cards came tumbling down. It should come as no surprise that the individuals who make up these companies have the exact same problems as their companies. Many people's lives are also a house of cards, an illusion. If major corporations are having problems, *you* shouldn't be embarrassed to have financial problems. However, there is no 700-billion-dollar bailout for you. You have to help yourself.

Visualize Change

Are you where you want to be financially? If you're not open to change, you want to stay exactly where you are. Truth is truth.

To change your path, seek motivation to begin the journey. As you do the work contained in this book, you will begin to see change. You will be better equipped to recognize the path you are on and begin to understand and enjoy it.

This book is a stepping-stone to understanding different aspects of your life. It is really about reprogramming your brain. The data you are using might have come to you when you were seven years old. You are not seven years old anymore; it is time to reassess the information you absorbed when you were young.

We have all unconsciously downloaded misinformation into our brains. We now have to consciously begin identifying our early money programming memories and work to change those beliefs. You have picked up this book—and possibly others like it—so you have already started the process of self-discovery. The more I've learned about myself, the more I've understood the impact that even the most seemingly insignificant events have had on my life.

As you read the following chapters, you will have many opportunities to visualize your own future. The exercises have been created to help you reframe your own financial life. You will get the most out of this book by spending the time necessary to visualize and complete each exercise.

I believe that one of the most important ways to bring about change is through visualization. This technique involves envisioning your future as you want it to be (rather than as your current reality). You may see yourself with an abundance of money or paid up on all your credit card debt or driving a new car. If you can't visualize how your future could be, it is difficult to believe you can take the necessary steps to get there.

When you visualize, let go of negative judgments of yourself. Picture the person you would like to be. Visualize this person fully and completely. We often stop ourselves from becoming our "best self" with worry and fear, which actually stalls forward movement of any kind. The point is not to fix yourself; the point is to embrace yourself.

Perhaps you'd like to be an NBA basketball player, but you realize you may be too old or too short to make it. Maybe you could be an announcer or recruiter. Maybe you could find another way to become connected to the sport. Look at your dreams and put them into the context of reality. Accept your limitations without labeling them as bad. And if there is a way to expand your limitations, all the better.

You may look at some people and think they live a charmed life. Those same people may, in turn, look at you and think you are the one who has it together. I work with some clients whom others consider to be extremely fortunate. Here's the reality: they are not any different than you. In fact, you may be in a better place financially than they are.

Part of my reason for writing this book is to let you know that it's not just you having financial difficulties. You are not alone. Don't apologize for what you are about to uncover. Other people have money problems. How do I know? Because people trust me with their financial truth. It's hard to lie to your accountant. There are people with money and people without money, and you can't always tell them apart. Numbers don't lie, but people do. Trust me, I know.

So don't apologize for your vision or for the things you want. Some of us have been taught that it is selfish to want more money or a nicer car. You have every right to want to fix your finances and to live in abundance.

How to Use This Book

I've organized the following chapters to give you information you'll use to complete a series of exercises. The exercises are designed to help you identify your own Money Nerve. It is best to read each chapter and work through the exercises before moving to the next chapter. Take your time. Many of the exercises will draw on your abilities to visualize both your past and your future. Some will ask you to delve deeply into your relationships. Some will cause you to confront your worst financial fears. All of them are crucial components to identifying your Money Nerve—and lead you down paths that will help you gain control of your finances and create your own definition of financial success.

1

Set a New Course

The Money Nerve

IT'S TIME TO CREATE THE NEW FINANCIAL you. You are ready to leave the past behind and confront your financial fears. Great news! You've already taken the first step. You are reading this book to get new information and new tools to potentially make profound changes in your financial situation and your relationship with money.

Before you start any journey, you need to know where you want to go (your goal), what you have to work with (your beliefs), and what new things you will bring (your new perspective). The first portion of this book explores your story through other people's stories. It's important to bring your story to consciousness so that you begin to take responsibility for where you are. This, in turn, helps you make clearer choices that will take you where you want to go—and allow you to realize your own power.

Embrace your story; own your story. Be willing to accept that you might be partially responsible for your current state of affairs. Be willing to make necessary adjustments to get where you really want to be. Whether you want to have millions of dollars, own lots of property, travel, save for a Jacuzzi, or stop bouncing checks, you need to acknowledge your goals. After that, you must make the commitment to go for it.

In this chapter, we look at a couple of personal Money Nerve stories that illustrate how dramatically our finances are impacted when our Money Nerve is pinched. We'll see how those people took control of their financial fears by making different choices that better reflected what they actually wanted to have in their lives. We then look at mental mapping, the way in which we have programmed ourselves to think.

Understanding your mental map and learning to make adjustments to it is an important part of this book. Once you get an idea about how mental mapping works, you will have the chance to look at your process and start questioning what you really want … and whether you are willing to make the changes to get it. At the end of the chapter, you'll find exercises that will help you identify your mental map. Be honest without being judgmental. Let's jump in.

Rich Mind, Poor Body

Andrea fell in love and moved away with her boyfriend, whom she eventually married. He grew up in a very wealthy family in which money was treated as disposable. Consequently, he was irresponsible with money. When money came in, he spent it like he was still a wealthy person—even though, most of the time, he was broke. He was an artist and felt his actions were consistent with being an artist. He was often a month and a half late with the rent and other bills. And then, unexpectedly, he would sell a painting for fifteen grand, pay the bills, and say, "I'm going to the Bahamas." They would live it up for two months and then find themselves back in the same situation, unable to keep up with their bills.

Andrea said, "He always had a *no worries* attitude, and it stressed me out like crazy!" She realized that, for her to have more money and more control, she needed to go back to school. She borrowed money for school and completed her education to enable her to earn a decent income. Eventually, the stress of their financial situation was too much for Andrea, and it contributed to their divorce.

Andrea took back control of her financial situation by budgeting so that she knew exactly how much money she needed to pay bills and cover expenses each month. Once she knew what had to be paid, she knew how much money she needed to make. She worked freelance and took every job thrown her way. No job was too small. If she earned more money than she had needed the prior month, she put the extra into savings and pretended it did not exist. The next month, she planned on how much money she needed to earn without factoring in the extra money. That way, if she were ever in a pinch, she had a rainy day fund.

Now she is married to a man who is much more in alignment with her financial perspective. He is more practical with his money, and she is much more comfortable because they share the same financial goals and strategies.

Faith Will Provide

John's father was a devout Christian and a pastor of a small church. It was a point of pride that the Lord always provided, even if John's family didn't have a lot of money. Almost without fail, when winter came, a member of the church would approach him and say, "The Lord has put it in my heart to buy your kids winter coats." Thus, the family would get winter coats. John's parents trusted God to take care of the family, and they were always taken care of—just not on John's timetable.

When John was young, his family had a tradition: if you were passed a dime and needed the dime, it was yours; but if you didn't need to spend it, it should be passed to someone else who might need it. They called it living on faith. Looking back, John realized that, as an adult, he hated counting on people because, as a child, he had no control over whether his wants and needs were met. While the experience did not lessen his faith, it did help him recognize that he wanted a more active role in his financial road map.

The fun part here is that Andrea and John are now married to each other. They traveled different roads to arrive at a similar point of view. Because they each had a solid belief system about money and very real models for how they *didn't* want to live, they were able to move confidently and securely into their financial future together.

How Money Nerves Differ

There are two important pieces of information in these stories. First, neither Andrea nor John blamed the artist or the minister for their different ways of seeing things. Each belief system worked for the artist and the minister, they just didn't work for Andrea or John.

We all have different wants and needs. Some people have a strong desire to save for the future. Others want to live in the moment. We all have different levels of emotional tolerance toward our present financial situation. If your Money Nerve is being pinched, explore ways to release the tension.

Start to question your core emotional impulses when certain money situations come up. How do you react to an overdrawn bank account, seeing your newest credit card statement, writing big checks, creating a budget, buying something on an impulse? Do you always need to pay for dinner? Do you feel scared, empowered, ashamed, proud, angry?

Maybe you spend money to cover insecurities. Maybe you use money to manipulate (for example, hinting to relatives that they stand to inherit large sums if they are in good stead with you). Maybe you give away money to feel empowered. This is your journey. What emotions come up for you when you think about money?

The second important piece of information is that our financial maps—the mental maps we follow whenever we deal with finances—are about choice. Andrea and John both chose to be more active in their finances and to take personal responsibility for what they had and did not have.

If you want to rely on faith or an impulse, go for it—but realize this book is probably not for you. This book is for people who feel their Money Nerve and want to be in the driver's seat.

Mental Mapping

Finding Your Way

When I first moved to Los Angeles, I assumed the fastest way to travel was getting on the interstate. But instead of getting on the fastest route, I ran into bumper-to-bumper traffic. Still, I was comfortable with where the road was going. There were buffer lanes, no potholes, no twists or turns … and I knew I would eventually get where I wanted to go. Fifty thousand other people were thinking the same thing, and none of us ever really got up to speed.

When you have a map, there are several routes to the same destination. This book will guide you on your personal financial journey with the help of a mental map. According to *A Dictionary of Geography,*[1] "[A] mental map is a map of the environment within the mind of an individual which reflects the knowledge and prejudices of that individual." You will identify your current mental financial position (or beliefs) and envision where you ultimately want to end up. Once you understand your financial mental state, it is much easier to determine how you can adjust your route to get you to your new financial destination. You can change your mental map perceptions with the knowledge you'll obtain in this book. Becoming aware of

---

1   "Mental Map." *A Dictionary of Geography.* Second ed. New York: Oxford University Press, 1997. 277. Print.

your mental map helps you recognize how you unconsciously divert yourself from your ultimate destination.

Once you are aware of where you sabotage yourself financially, you can begin to change your automatic responses. As you start to consciously hear yourself creating roadblocks, you will be able to consciously reroute your mind to the course you have set for yourself.

Mental mapping your approach toward finances means rerouting the I-can't-afford-it mentality. I like the word *mapping* because we are all on a path. No path leads the wrong way. Are you taking the scenic route to your financial destination? It might take you three times as long to get there, but that doesn't mean you won't have a beautiful journey.

Interstate Mentality

If you have an interstate mentality toward finances, the only traffic that exists is in your head. On an actual freeway, you can see hundreds of cars ahead of you on the road. The roadblocks you have set up in your mind tend to be less obvious. Nobody is setting out an orange cone with blinking lights telling you to merge your credit card debt.

An interstate mentality takes place when you try to juggle payments on seven credit cards, transfer money from one bank account to another, free up expenses on one credit card so you can charge more on it while you make a payment for another card, and wait for a paycheck to cover checks you just wrote.

If you have a lot of different things going on financially, you have to stop to take a breath. Be aware of all the different moving parts of your financial journey. You can't keep your foot on the gas pedal and think that you don't have to worry about where you're headed. If you move too fast and stay too busy, you can lose track of your destination. With more going on, there are increased chances you'll get off your path and end up in an accident.

Slow down and make conscious choices. "I won't charge my credit card, I'll just skip going out to dinner this week." "Maybe I really don't need three new outfits." "I should balance my checkbook." "Take a breath and focus." (It's good to remind yourself to slow down.)

If you're driving down the freeway and everyone puts their brakes on, you need to be aware of the shift in traffic. On the scenic route, you can fall off a cliff or forget to stop for gas. If you're too tired, you might fall asleep at the wheel. You need to make conscious choices in your financial travels and stay aware of your surroundings … regardless of the speed you choose.

Financial GPS

When we get in a car and activate the GPS, we assume it knows where we are and will get us where we want to go. Yet from experience, we know we can't always rely on it to be accurate. In order to make good decisions before going anywhere, we first need to know where we are and where we want to go. Similarly, to make good financial decisions, we need to break the GPS mentality and start thinking for ourselves instead of staying on financial autopilot. My college was near the Mississippi River. I had a friend who had lived near the river his entire life, and he did not know which way was east! In Los Angeles, I tell people which way is west all the time—I tell them to let the Pacific Ocean be their guide.

You may believe that your financial advisor and your accountant use some kind of financial GPS to get you where you want to go. Even if they do, you are ultimately the driver of your financial vehicle. I have several clients who, in the face of grave consequences, have driven right off a financial cliff despite having been informed of its presence. Collectively, most of us have become unconscious. You, as a reader of this book, are working your way out of that dream state. After you have applied the information in this book, you might begin helping other people approach their finances more consciously.

Create a New Mental Map

Two different people could be riding next to each other in a convertible car with the roof down. One might be thinking, "I love the wind in my hair. This is the life." The other might be thinking, "There is no roof over my head. This is so dangerous. I can't wait to get out of this death trap." They are both experiencing the convertible, but their mental mapping is worlds apart.

You can create a new mental map about money that will help you move toward your financial goals. Your current mental map might tell you that you can't enjoy your present lifestyle if you don't keep using credit cards. You don't care what the interest rate is. You could be paying 20 or 30 percent on your credit card. If you curbed your expenses, that interest percentage could buy you a new car or a trip to Italy. Someone else's mental map might tell them the only way they can have a better life is to stop using credit cards completely.

The Power of Words

What Fuels Your Mind?

Words are powerful. Think before you speak. Listen to what you are actually saying and start to identify what you say consciously. You can't change where you want to be if you don't know where you are. I hear people say, "I need a TV," or they say, "I need to go to Hawaii." But those statements are not true. They are *wants,* not *needs.* They want those things. They need oxygen; they don't need the newest cell phone. Once you start to hear your own voice, you can begin to give yourself alternative choices, which will change your mental map.

Little words can be more powerful than we realize. For example, the word *but* indicates a contrast or exception, and it can also negate everything that precedes it. Many of my clients say, "I want financial success, but I am afraid of it," or they say, "I want to learn healthy financial habits, but my folks never taught me about money," or even, "I want to stand up for myself, but people might criticize me." That one little word packs lots of negative power. I have worked to eliminate the word as much as possible and replace it with the word *and*. Using the word *and* allows both situations to exist. It lets you have your fear while also feeling empowered. See if you can hear the difference. "I want financial success, and I am afraid of it," or say, "I want to learn healthy financial habits, and my folks never taught me about money," or state, "I want to stand up for myself, and people might criticize me." You can be overwhelmed by your finances and still move forward with change. Be aware of the words you use. Making tiny changes can shift your views in powerful ways.

Listen to what you say about your finances. "I want to have financial freedom, but I'm broke." You can reword that slightly: "I want to have financial freedom, *and* I'm in a financially hard place right now, *and* I'm working toward eliminating that debt." You might hear yourself say, "I want to have money in the bank, but I have lots of debt." Replace that in a positive way by saying, "I'm working toward financial freedom, *and* I'm eliminating debt along the way."

Are You Really Sorry?

Do you apologize for speaking your mind? There's no need to if you do so respectfully—you're just being clear about where you stand. I have a friend who used to apologize to me constantly. She apologized for things that happened to me that she had nothing to do with. If I lost ten dollars, she would apologize. She even apologized for apologizing. I finally made a deal with her: every time she apologized to me, she had to give me a dollar. The first few weeks we were together, I ate breakfast, lunch, and dinner on her dime, her dollar.

When she started realizing how much she was handing over to me, she became focused. She began stopping herself. She stopped the automatic pilot in her head and thought about what she was saying. She would say instead, "Oh how interesting." Or she would say, "I wonder how that happened?" She changed her mental map of always being responsible for things she was not responsible for. She thanks me to this day for pointing it out, and I appreciate that she's no longer sorry. Changing her mental map took financial incentive.

Brake, Break, Broke

What words are you using that negatively affect your relationship with money? If you say, "I'm broke," stop to consider whether or not you are really broke. Are you going to a soup kitchen and living on the street?

The next time you have the impulse to say, "I am broke," "I can't do that," "I have no money, so that isn't going to happen," stop and create a mental space for yourself. Start to mentally identify the true scenario and eventually replace your words with different options.

You (to yourself): *I'm broke.*

You (to yourself): *I'm broke.*

You (to yourself): *I'm bro ... I choose to spend money on shoes.*

You (to yourself): *I'm br ... I choose to not save for my retirement.*

You (to yourself): *I'm ... I'm making better choices with my money.*

Instead of saying you are broke, replace those words with, "I am someone who eats out or wears nice clothes instead of having money in the bank." After all, you are making the choices that lead to not having money, and you are not broke. Take back your power to choose.

One couple called me in tears because, in their words, they were "beyond broke." Earlier, the husband had decided that buying and reselling boats would be a good business. Having owned a boat myself, I recognized the economy was not ideal and told him it probably wasn't a good time to buy. He did it anyway, and that decision resulted in thousands of dollars being tied up in several boats.

The couple was about to be evicted from their apartment just when they were expecting a baby. I asked them how big their biggest boat was, and

I learned it was the size of a small apartment. I asked them why they weren't living on the boat. They said that if they lived on a boat, people would think they were poor or unsuccessful. I told them I lived on my boat for over three years and loved it. I also reminded them that they were about to be evicted and didn't want to ruin their credit. The simple solution was clear to me.

The couple's mental map indicated that living on a boat was a sign of failure. It could have said, "We're on an adventure. How amazing is this?" Their mental map indicated that moving out of a rental apartment reflected on them poorly. It could have said, "Hey, cool, one less expense to deal with." They finally agreed that moving onto the boat was their best choice—and that they weren't "beyond broke." They allowed their mental map to shift.

Be Conscious of What You Say

Choose your words consciously. Many clients tell me how broke they are. They repeat their automatic story without thinking about what they are saying. If I know that they recently returned from a trip or bought a new car or recently received a weekly massage, I call them on it. I suggest that maybe they are not broke; rather, their priorities don't match their desires. And for a brief moment, they may stop and listen to what I am saying—and they might even acknowledge that they are not really broke. This is the first step.

What you say out loud is the greatest indication of your mental mapping. If you can't hear what you are saying, find a friend who will be happy to challenge you on what you say you want or what you say your current state is.

Stories We Learned at School

Most of us are trained to tell ourselves a certain story from the time we are young. We go to school and learn what to say and do. We wear the right clothes and say the right things so that we fit in and follow the norm. And then we start limiting our own unique thoughts. By the time we become adults, our conformity causes us to carry on a charade of thinking we all have our act together. But for many, it is just an act!

In grade school, I was taught *not* to raise my hand to answer a question. I knew the answer, but most of the kids would harass me as a know-it-all. And it didn't matter if my parents told me not to worry about it—they didn't have to survive in my classroom.

A lesson far too many students learn is that they are only okay if they wear the right clothes, drive the right car, and eat the right food. They don't want to wear a no-name shirt because they're only supposed to wear shirts with the latest popular logos. If they wear the wrong shoes, everyone will assume they are poor. If they're eligible for the school lunch program, they'll hide their ticket so that the other kids won't think their parents are losers. If their parents are considered failures, they are considered failures. Financial pressure to maintain images of wealth have been so strongly instilled in our country's kids that some are even willing to kill other kids for their tennis shoes.[2]

There is truth to the quote attributed to Theodore Roosevelt that "comparison is the thief of joy." As an adult, you may now recognize that no one has the right to impose his or her judgment on you when your principles differ or when you follow your own eclectic style. You can train yourself out of the unconscious collective. You can learn to break the pattern of repeating the same story to yourself that you learned in school. The words to that story may have had a more powerful and lasting effect on you than you realize.

Choose Another Direction

How do you shift the impulse to say, "I'm broke," "I want to be rich," "I need to win the lottery"? The answer has nothing to do with obtaining the million dollars that exists in some fictitious bank in the middle of the universe. It has everything to do with your commitment to choose your own reality.

---

2   Rick Telander, "Senseless," *Sports Illustrated,* May 14, 1990.

I am a person who tends to say *yes* more than *no*. It is a calculated *yes*, and it tends to keep me moving forward. Do you allow yourself to say, "I am open to the possibility"? Most people are in a *no* mode. If you are in a *no* mode, you are in a *no move* mode. You won't get far with a negative mentality. Momentarily create a place of goodwill and generosity for yourself.

Become someone who says, "Yes! It is possible that I am capable of handling my own finances." "Yes! I am ready to take charge of my financial life." "Yes! I am prepared to be conscious." "Yes! I am overwhelmed and want to stop reading this book." Acknowledge the feeling and keep moving forward; there is work to do. I never said this was going to be easy—shifting direction is not easy.

When we are challenged to change, the effects can be physical. For example, as a stand-up comedian, I feel the challenge of the moment in my gut. I feel sick to my stomach every time I get on stage to perform stand-up comedy. I love to do it, though, so I don't mind working through the difficulty.

No matter how you deal with change, wouldn't you love to see positive monthly balances in your checking account? Wouldn't it be nice to know that your future was secure? Start looking for the destination you'd like to reach on your own mental map. Once you know where you want to go, the words you use to tell yourself about the journey you want to take will start shaping it into reality.

Take the First Step

Daily Mental Mapping

Take a notepad and jot down your schedule for the upcoming day. Be sure to set aside thirty minutes for personal time. If you can't take quiet time for thirty minutes, you can start with fifteen minutes (or even five minutes). This is vital. You need to create a mental space for yourself. If you have kids or feel like you don't have any time available, just try it for one week.

Simply sit and do nothing. Be quiet and create enough mental space in your life to start listening to your own thoughts. Turn the phone off and keep yourself off limits to anyone else's needs. Most of us are so busy that we struggle to be present. Mahatma Gandhi used to regularly sit in contemplation for an hour—and even longer when the demands were greater. He once said, "I have so much to accomplish today that I must meditate for two hours instead of one."[3]

Let's say an attic is your storage space right now ... and that you have always wanted to play an instrument or be a painter or be a writer. Now you have this big attic, but it has too much clutter to be useful. Your mind is like that attic. Every day, your job is to sit in silence and clear out your mental attic. You also need to create a safe physical space, inside or out, which is your sanctuary. Your physical space could be your bedroom, half of your garage, or even a piece of carpet that you pull out and sit on. In that physical space, you get to do whatever you want. You can be messy, you can be goofy, or you can just sit in silence.

Spending time by yourself gives you the ability to hear your own voice and discover your dreams. Einstein said, "Imagination is everything. It is the preview of life's coming attractions." With a certain amount of quiet time, you start to listen with the ears behind your ears. You may hear voices saying, "Only special people do that," "I don't deserve it"— and the voices may not be your own. It will sound like you are saying it, but if you are like me, you might hear your parents telling you that you are not capable. Tell those voices to be quiet; you are busy. And then go back and pay attention to your own voice.

Ask yourself where you would like to be in one year or five years. Would you like to be free of credit card debt? Would you like to have traveled the world? Would you like to have put away money in a retirement account? Would you like to change your spending habits? Would you

---

3   Tom Barrett, "A Healthier Routine." (2002): n. page. Accessed October 4, 2012. http://www.interluderetreat.com/meditate/7things.htm.

like to see 50,000 dollars in savings? Once you know where you would like to be, state your goal. A year from now, I'd like to stop using credit cards. In five years, I'd like to be credit card debt free. A year from now, I want to go to school for additional training. In five years, I'd like to be in another career or own my own company.

Quiet the censor in your mind and just let your imagination travel where it likes. After allowing yourself this quiet time every day, you may be surprised to see where your imagination takes you!

Start to Question

A little boy started saving his allowance and any spare change he found, stashing it under his pillow. One night, the little boy asked his father, "How much money do you make?" The father was offended and told his son it was none of his business. Later, he started feeling guilty and went back to his son and apologized. He said, "Son, I make twenty dollars an hour. And I'm curious, why do you ask?" His son looked at him and said, "I know you are very busy and have so much to do. I want to know how much you make so I can save my money and buy an hour of your time."

You may recognize that time is valuable, but what value would you put on financial freedom? If you place a high value on financial freedom, you can start mentally paying yourself to take action. Imagine yourself getting a check after you take the time to mental map. Or if you prefer, make sure you give yourself a reward for your efforts—even if it's a small gesture.

Your awareness of each step you take and your process of starting to question things will help you make the shift. As you walk through life, breathe deeply enough to create a space that will allow you to objectively make a choice, rather than simply reacting. This is hard to do. It is hard to get out of autopilot and navigate on your own. Be good to yourself during this process. Have empathy with yourself.

When Will You "Arrive"?

I have always believed that there would come a point in my life when I was going to affect lives in a positive way. I knew I wasn't ready—until one day when I woke up thinking, *I better get ready.* I knew I had better get ready for the moment the opportunity would come. Maybe that would be in twenty years, and I wasn't worried about that. I didn't have a timetable. I just knew that I should get on my path, and that preparation would be part of the journey. A person can make amazing advances … even if others are unable to see the results. Start your journey now and don't worry about when you will arrive.

When I was in India and Spain, buildings that took hundreds of years to complete amazed me. The structures were designed for future generations to enjoy. The builders did not expect instant gratification. You are building your financial future. The journey to that financial future can be as beautiful and exciting as any other amazing project. It just doesn't happen overnight—and it doesn't have to be painful and devoid of encouraging milestones.

Time to Change

You have read some personal stories. You have started to look at your mental map. You have begun to question your emotional beliefs and attachments around money. Are you ready to take action?

If you hate your job, find your passion and work in that field. If you don't have skills, take classes. If you hate being broke, start saving. If you are unhappy with your debt, make a plan to pay it down while curbing spending. What is working for you and what isn't? Are you ready to start creating your financial freedom even if the process is scary? This is where you begin to head in a new direction.

Call to Action

Your Mental Map

Start a Money Nerve journal to write in daily. Answer the Call to Action questions in it, as well.

1. Record your mental mapping discoveries in your journal by answering this question: what has your inner voice revealed to you regarding money?

2. Record three things you have heard yourself say out loud relating to money in the last few days.

3. Do you still have the same beliefs about money that you held as a child?

4. What did your mother teach you about money? Your father?

5. What core beliefs do you still hold regarding money? Do they serve you?

6. Does gender play a role in your current money belief system? If so, how?

7. Identify your current story.

8. Reread your answers to the above questions and write down areas of painful financial realizations and promising financial realizations.

9. If you could tell a young adult the truth about money, what would you say?

2

Explore Your Money Nerve

Which Emotions Trigger Your Money Nerve?

THE PURPOSE OF THIS BOOK IS TO guide you toward a healthy relationship with your money, regardless of how much you have. A friend of mine once told me that success consists of three things—and most people forget about the third. Success encompasses knowing what is available, what you want, and what you are going to do once you get what you want. If your only goal is to be rich, your goal may not be specific enough. A GPS is no good unless you plug in a destination. How can your finances get on board if you don't really know where you are going? Being rich is not a destination.

Many of us view success as a destination. Success is a word that has no single definition. Some would define success as having enough money to travel on vacations a couple of times per year. Others may define success as never having to work again. This chapter will help you become aware of the Money Nerve that may be keeping you from attaining your specific financial goals.

As you read the examples in this chapter, take note of similar emotional reactions you may have in your financial life. As you become more adept at recognizing when your Money Nerve begins to surface, you will become more conscious of its existence. By becoming more aware, you can start to take control and empower your financial life.

Two people can take the same action, but each person might have a completely different motive for what he or she is doing. For example, in the last chapter, we talked about two people's experience of driving in a convertible with the top down. From afar, you see two people in a convertible. One of them may have grown up taking road trips with his or her parents and thinks it's fun. The other may have had a bad experience or accident that causes him or her to be afraid. Even though their outside experience is the same, their inner experience is completely different. It's often easy to define an action, yet it's harder to determine the reasoning behind the emotions that that action stirs up.

Emotions explain the intention. I've had several clients who took out stated loans (otherwise known as *liar loans*.) At the time, they didn't really think they were lying, but if they had done an accurate personal financial inventory, they would have realized that they could never make the payments in the first place. They were essentially lying to themselves. Many people who took out liar loans were so frustrated that others around them were buying homes that they lied to the bank in order to buy their own. Their lie eventually resulted in feelings of shame when they were unable to make their payments—and of anger toward their worsened financial situation. From little white lies to fraud, there are a number of emotions behind why one tells a financial lie.

Throughout life, your emotions continually evolve. Moments of heightened emotion are triggers to help you realize your emotional makeup has changed. What might cause you to react with anger at a young age might make you laugh now. You're not going to see happiness as the main driver in this chapter because positive emotions are generally not motivators to get out of financial difficulties. Most adults having money issues are dealing with negative emotions. When I have clients in my office who are doing well financially, they are generally upbeat and positive.

The following list of emotions that can trigger your Money Nerve is not a complete list—consider it a starting point for self-examination.

Exhaustion

There are dozens of emotions that surface when it comes to money. When I was thinking back on the emotions I have dealt with in client meetings over the years, I came up with an exhaustive list. Looking at the root cause of our financial actions can be exhausting. Being broke can be exhausting. Budgeting can be exhausting.

Many people have a message in their mind stuck on replay, and it says, *I don't want to look at my financial reality. I just don't want to look at how messed up I actually am.* It sometimes seems less exhausting to live in a make-believe world! The problem with that assumption is that it is make-believe. As soon as you get an overdraft fee, you may feel de-energized or deflated.

Elizabeth just received a large settlement from a lawsuit, and I agreed to help her work through the first few steps necessary to get her financial life in order. She had known for about two years that she would be receiving a large sum of money, and once she had that knowledge, she let her finances take a back seat. So for two years, she didn't deal with her money issues because she knew they would eventually be resolved. She came to see me one day, and she looked like she had been in another accident. Elizabeth had become emotionally exhausted because of her finances. She had been receiving calls from creditors, and she was ignoring them because she was waiting for her money to come through. She was almost numb to the daily phone calls from creditors and the IRS.

Some people are so exhausted by their constant financial difficulties that they wrongly believe that some outside force must take over in order for real financial change to occur. As is often the case, finances continue to be difficult, and the windfall never arrives. In Elizabeth's case, the money eventually came, but for others, the lack of change itself is exhausting. If you are unwilling to take action to change your situation, you may find yourself financially exhausted and depressed.

Turn your exhaustion around:

- Analyze your true situation. Elizabeth should not have counted on money that hadn't yet arrived.

- Create a strategy to move in a new direction. Elizabeth could have called her creditors to negotiate a payment plan based on the fact that her settlement was coming soon. She could have faxed them proof that she would soon receive a large settlement.

Depression

I have seen many people—poor and wealthy alike—go through personal financial depression. I have had clients who walked away from their homes, knowing their mortgage arm was going to adjust in the next few years. Some of them looked like they had aged a decade over the course of two or three years due to the financial pressures they were dealing with.

During a personal financial depression, many people take no action and stop paying their bills. The common denominator for these depressed clients is that they assumed their financial situation would continue exactly the same as it had in the past. They had no contingency plan. Many clients explained that they did not plan for the future because they didn't want to jinx their current success.

I have never agreed with this mentality. I see a contingency plan as a bank account of confidence. Thinking you will be successful is much easier to do when you are not worried about paying your rent. Having a contingency plan gives you the ability to focus on goals that are months or years away (instead of dealing with an ever-present financial depression).

The other key to fighting your way out of a depression is to make sure that you have a support structure. A support structure could be a formal group of people from different fields who meet monthly to hold each other accountable for goals they're trying to reach. It might be a group of friends who agree to be supportive of each other. It could be a life coach. It could be one or two individuals you can be open with.

Be careful not to alienate your support structure by constantly reflecting on the negative. Bill has been without a source of income for about two years, and he is now in the midst of a severe financial depression. I was speaking with a mutual friend who said he feels so drained after a five-minute conversation with Bill that he dreads taking his calls. Bill is an interesting, talented, and funny guy, but none of his positive sides are shining through.

Has your financial depression evoked negativity in you? Imagine what you must seem like to the people you deal with on a regular basis. If you find yourself in a negative state or find you are pushing people away, make a proactive choice to pull yourself out of your misery. Make a list of all the positive things you have in your life right now, such as your financial achievements (my car is paid off, my credit card debt is reduced). Or spend a day without any expenses: sit in a park, go hiking, get out in nature, shift your environment. Volunteer at a soup kitchen and see people who really struggle to put your own situation in perspective.

Talking about your financial depression can be a tricky thing to do. One of my clients recently dealt with his financial difficulties through humor. His car was stolen, and he lost his phone, so he decided to throw a virtual pity party. He invited some of his friends on Facebook to attend. He made a joke out of a financially depressing situation, and about one hundred of his friends joined in. They posted hilarious comments because they didn't have to deal with him face-to-face. It made him laugh, and it released some of the sadness he was feeling. In addition, he was able to honestly share with others who could be of further support to him in the future.

I realize that dealing with financial problems can be exhausting and depressing. Sometimes, bringing a little levity to the situation can be helpful. It can be hard to laugh at a depressing situation, and without allowing yourself to take a quick mental break, you can easily find yourself feeling overwhelmed.

Turn your depression around:

- Have a contingency plan.

- Create or draw on a support network.

- Find a way to view your situation with humor.

Overwhelmed

It's important to consider the pace you set to achieve your financial goals. If you set an unrealistic pace, you're more likely to become overwhelmed.

When I first arrived at Lukla, Nepal and prepared to make my ascent to Mount Everest Base Camp, my goal was ten days and over nine thousand vertical feet away. I would have been kidding myself to think it could be done all at once.

Initially, the plan was to climb about one thousand feet in altitude, acclimate, and continue to the top incrementally. The first couple of days were pretty extreme. The thought of hiking ten hours per day over a difficult, seemingly endless path was overwhelming. My group started to convince itself that it was too difficult and considered turning back.

I wasn't having it. I set my watch and told my group that we would only focus on hiking for one hour with a water break at thirty minutes. We would not even talk about an eight-hour hike or what the rest of the day looked like. We wouldn't talk about what ifs (for example, what if it gets dark? What if something terrible happens?). Everyone agreed to hike for only one hour and focus only on that one hour.

Once we had gotten a few one-hour hikes under our belts with water breaks on the half hour, the group members stopped needing to take a break every thirty minutes. They felt they could easily continue, and they wanted to keep hiking for longer chunks of time. I remember one day specifically when the peak seemed miles and miles away. Because of our false perception, it appeared unreachable. So I set my watch for an hour, and we started hiking. Within forty-five minutes, we had arrived. It was actually closer than we realized.

In the same way, financial security may seem like it is unattainable, but you may simply be in need of a little perspective. The cure for being financially overwhelmed is persistence and knowledge. The way to a savings account is one step at a time. Put away ten dollars per paycheck knowing that, over time, that will add up to a large sum. In that way, you can create a new habit.

If you have an area of finances that overwhelms you, surround yourself with books on the subject or go online to reputable sites. If you are more inclined to a discussion, try to find people who are strong in your area of weakness.

Financial stability may not happen overnight. By setting goals and starting the journey, you may find that you are only a short distance away from relief. Just put one foot in front of the other and get moving.

Turn your overwhelming feelings around:

- Persist.

- Know where you are and where you are going.

- Learn the financial terrain.

Fear

What are you waiting for? Are you still in the same spot?! For most people, the idea of climbing Mount Everest is scary. The thought of walking along a narrow trail with a three-thousand-foot cliff at its edge may leave you frozen in your tracks. It is literally freezing up there! Most of my adult life has been spent confronting that which I fear most, one item after another. I have finally arrived at a point where I live with minimal fear—and I still have occasional bouts of thoughts of financial fear. I fear a lack of money in my bank account. If I don't have enough money to cover three months of expenses, I start to worry. I get butterflies in my stomach. I look at my bank account not just for my own sake—I have employees and other responsibilities to think about when it comes to my money.

The most successful people I know are always active. They try new forms of exercise and food; they read books and attend seminars. They are always on the lookout for a new way of thinking to stay innovative. They may not be successful in every venture they undertake, but they have so many irons in the fire that one eventually gets hot.

Financial fear can make you stop in your tracks. Not taking a look at your account balances, not making any decisions, ignoring your family, and disregarding your financial advisor are a few examples of how people start to freeze up.

Moving forward doesn't require a huge step. Every so often, I organize everything in my life: my garage, my medicine cabinet, my finances. I do a personal inventory. A personal inventory helps me clean out what I don't need, mentally and otherwise. When I take inventory, I have a much better idea of where I am and what I have. This gives me structure and an awareness of what I may be lacking. Every six months or so, I go through my previous budget and look at my finances with fresh eyes. To continually make strides, you have to regularly take inventory in all areas of your life. You may be living with fears that no longer make sense.

I know many people who are afraid their whole financial life is going to fall apart at any minute. Sometimes, their fear does not correlate to their financial reality. My friend's grandfather invented a very popular ice cream treat. The sweet invention earned his family millions of dollars. His parents grew up during World War II, and his parents' conversation was always about how they were going to be thrown out onto the streets at any moment. Their fear was irrational. They had several maids, ten cars, and a mansion. So my friend grew up thinking, *We're going to end up on the streets.* It wasn't until he got older that he realized his mindset was based on an irrational fear.

Until recent years, America's younger generation did not live in fear of losing it all. They grew up in an era of abundance. They had no concept of scarcity. Now, when they see their friends losing jobs and having to give up their houses, they start to live in fear themselves. There is an increasing fear of the changing times and a potential lack of resources. In the current economic reality, many people I interact with on a daily basis are afraid of losing everything they have worked for.

My sister is a high school counselor in California. On a regular basis, students enter her office and tell her their parents are losing their homes. Several dozen students are transferring out because their parents have lost their jobs. People who had two good incomes six months prior are sleeping in the living room of a family member's house. Their fear is a reality. Similar stories are being told and retold across the country, and they are starting to affect the listeners on an emotional level. There is definitely a tangible increase in financial fears right now.

In order to combat your fears, make your choices when you are at your best. Don't go to the grocery store when you are starving. If you do, you tend to make unnecessary purchases and overspend. In the same manner, it is evident to me that very few people prepare for tough times before they happen. It is difficult to think about having a contingency plan when things are going well, and it is important to have a cushion right now. I am surprised by the number of people who are in unstable positions with high debt, yet they are sold on the idea that they need to get the latest electronic device.

There has been an ever-increasing strain on all of our resources, and I think a certain amount of fear is justified. You, the reader of this book, are probably aware of various situations in your state, community, and household. So how do you start to deal with your legitimate financial fears? You face them.

Turn your fear around:

- Take personal inventory.

- Make your choices when you are at your best.

- Face your fears.

Shame

I realize that it is difficult to discuss your feelings of financial fear without a sense of shame. Behind closed doors, some clients open up about the shame they feel about their current financial situation. After doing so, they often say they feel as though a weight has been lifted. A private conversation is the only place where most people will even begin to admit that they are financially struggling and can't make their payments. This can be especially true with men. There may be something to the idea that men have trouble expressing their emotions.

Financial shame often comes from not living up to a certain ideal. It may be a false expectation or a false belief. You may think you should own a home and provide for all of your family's needs, but perhaps you lost your job and that is no longer possible. Many of us live with an illusion of the sort of person we should be (or what we should have) rather than being realistic and honest about our situation.

I think it is good to have a benchmark for what you consider a healthy financial relationship. For example, you may want to have 50,000 dollars in your savings account as your measure of being financial healthy. Nowhere is it written in stone that if you do not meet the benchmark you are a bad person. If you have 48,000 dollars in your savings account, you don't need to beat yourself up over the other 2,000 dollars.

Maybe you set your benchmark to be, "I must own my own business." If you succeed at owning your own business and stress out every night, it may be time to pick a new benchmark. A number of my clients have met the benchmark they set for themselves—and are doing everything they can to maintain that benchmark—but doing so often works to their detriment.

One of my clients was recently given the opportunity to return to his high-paying corporate job after years of being on his own and struggling. He turned down the offer because his mother was so proud that he had his own office. This client almost lost everything in an attempt to keep his mother proud of his independence. Not meeting expectations is not necessarily negative; it is the shame that you put on yourself that can be debilitating.

A lot of financial shame is tied into one's life perspective. My grandparents were hesitant to take money from the "system." Their generation felt much more shame if they had to accept welfare or food stamps from the government than the current generation.

A stand-up comedy friend recently told me that the government was paying him to write jokes. I didn't understand what he was saying at first, but then I realized he was excited that he could launch his dream of making it as a comedian through unemployment. In general, the younger generation sees unemployment as a support system that is available to be utilized.

As with other emotions that trigger your Money Nerve, shame can be a motivator. Therefore, it is important to take note of the context in which the emotions arise.

Turn your shame around:

- Share your fears to lighten your load.

- Evaluate others' expectations of you.

- Clarify your own expectations of yourself.

Guilt

Everybody works hard for every dollar they get, and everybody deserves all the good things that they have—yet some of us feel guilty about having money. Steve had hired some guys to install solar panels on his house. He moved his luxury car into his garage so that the contractors wouldn't see it. He felt bad that they had come to his house on a Sunday, and he didn't want to seem like a rich snob. Steve felt guilty about owning a new car because he assumed the workers would resent him. When they were done with the installation, they had to put a heavy piece of equipment in his garage. When he reluctantly opened his garage door, the contractor said, "What are you shying away from? If I had that Lexus, I would say, 'Look at my Lexus. I deserve it.'" Steve acknowledged, "I do deserve it, and I love it." It took someone else to help him stop feeling guilty.

I know a number of artists who have turned self-destructive because they feel guilty for making money. Some of these artists see money as a corrupting force. They believe they have to modify their artistic creation or sell out to serve a client or employer. Even artists need to eat; yet by subjecting their vision or craftsmanship to serve a commercial goal, they feel they are being corrupted by greed. In short, they are concerned that the purity of their artistic vision will suffer. These artists may ask themselves, *Why did I become successful when all these people who are so much more talented did not?*

An inordinate number of people feel guilty because they think they don't really deserve the pay scale they are at, and they see that more competent people around them aren't getting paid as much as they are. They feel like impostors. Susan Pinker's book, *The Sexual Paradox*, analyzes the research around this impostor syndrome. She claims that more than 70 percent of successful people think they got a lucky break.[4] They consistently ignore the fact that they pursued additional education, put in additional hours, or gained years of experience to attain their current positions. Of course, those steps *led* to their success. Pinker states:

> What differentiates impostor syndrome from garden-variety self-doubt is that the feelings may wane but never entirely disappear, regardless of accolades. The other difference is that like depression, arthritis, and osteoporosis, it's more often women who find that it's chronic.[5]

Our corporate culture still favors men who are better at bluffing their way through their doubts (and less likely to speak about them). Women, though no less competent, may feel more like impostors and doubt their competency.

Turn your guilt around:

- Celebrate your success.

- Make a list of what you've done to reach your goals and achieve success.

---

4   Pinker cites this research: Gail M. Matthews, "Impostor Phenomenon: Attributions for Success and Failure," paper presented at the American Psychological Association, Toronto, 1984.

5   Susan Pinker, *The Sexual Paradox: Men, Women, and the Real Gender Gap* (New York: Scribner, 2008),188.

Undeserving

I was recently walking with a friend in Marina del Rey, California. We were looking at all of the boats docked there. After strolling for a bit, I noticed that she kept scoffing at the larger yachts. When I asked her why she was doing that, she replied, "I am just wondering what type of people get to own these things." I said, "People like me." She thought I was kidding, and we just moved on.

Later, as I reflected on our conversation, I realized that, even though we were walking side by side, we were mentally traveling in opposite directions. She was moving away from owning a boat, and I was moving toward it. Having been a boat owner previously, it was simple for me to believe that I deserved to be a boat owner again.

There are many people who look at expensive items like yachts or expensive houses and truly believe they don't deserve them. This type of mentality goes back to mental mapping. If you feel as though you don't deserve to own a home, you most likely will not take the necessary steps toward that goal. You will not start saving for a down payment if you really believe you will never own a home. It all comes back to how you see yourself. If you appreciate yourself enough to feel that you deserve what you desire, you set yourself up for a possible win (remembering that it takes hard work to get there). Self-appreciation empowers you; without it, you may be fighting feelings of insecurity.

Turn your feelings of undeserving around:

- Work on appreciating yourself.

- List the top ten things you did well this year.

- Sincerely accept compliments.

Insecurity

When one of my early associates bought his first house, I overheard our boss tell him that he really needed to evaluate the people he was hanging out with. Our boss pointed out that his current set of friends would not be his future set of friends because they would start to be jealous and try to pull him down. At the time, I realized we were both surrounded by a bunch of people who were only happy at happy hours. They rushed out of work and into the bar, and they never made any effort to move forward. Even though that conversation wasn't meant for me, it had a powerful effect on me.

Have you considered the fact that you might not be actively seeking the most success possible for yourself because your whole social structure would have to change? You like where you are at socially, and maybe if you started to climb a little higher on the ladder of success, your friends would make fun of you. The people who hold you back may do so out of insecurity.

When I returned home from my first year at Rhodes College, some of my high school friends turned on me. Suddenly, I was "Mr. Scholarship." I was not boastful (or any different, really), and still my friends mocked me. Unfortunately, this is a story that plays out on a frequent basis. It was my personal achievements and newfound sense of confidence that made my friends feel insecure. The person who focuses on achieving and moving forward can be unaware that he or she is separating himself or herself from old friends.

If you are in that group and wish to go further, the insecurity of losing those friends may keep you from achieving your higher goals. Clearly, when it comes to networking, you want to surround yourself with individuals who are doing well in the area in which you wish to excel. If you are in one group and really want to explore another field of interest, you might maintain your silence until you get to a place where you feel safe expressing your wants and desires. Depending on the company you are keeping, it may be very difficult for you to do something as simple as make positive choices. Now that I am older and more secure, I limit my interactions with unsupportive people when I encounter them.

Even if you have friends who support your financial wins, the economy itself can cause insecurity. There are larger factors at play that are out of your control. It's amazing how many clients I have who are close to the edge. On the surface, they seem to have it made. The reality is that they're flipping out because they don't know where their next dollar is going to come from. For many, financial insecurity is a real thing. The economy, business cycles, and personal circumstances may all lead to financial insecurity.

The key to lessening financial insecurity often comes from truthful budgeting. The more honest the assessment, the more secure you will be in your position. You might be frustrated, but you will be aware of your financial truth.

Turn your insecurity around:

- Evaluate your social circle.

- Surround yourself with supportive friends.

- Budget truthfully so you know your financial position.

Frustration

Many people are financially frustrated because they feel they are capable of earning a good living … yet they are not. More often than not, the amount of money a person earns has less to do with that person's capabilities and more to do with how they understand the new paradigm. I see the success paradigm shifting from a loyal worker who stays in one position, working hard for a lifetime, toward the new idea of increasing personal viability and continually searching for new opportunities in new organizations and fields.

Financial institutions and banks have new sets of rules. In order to mitigate your frustration when applying for a loan, you should first study the working template. Ask the bank exactly what it is they are looking for, and then work within the boundaries of the new template to tell your financial history. I do not mean that you should disregard your ethics. The more knowledge you have about the working template, the more seamless your reporting will become—and the less frustrating the outcome.

I have a client who was looking for a line of credit from the bank. He had 20,000 dollars in his personal account and another 70,000 dollars in his business account. The bank would not extend him a line of credit because it wanted to see 50,000 dollars in his personal account. The client asked whether he could transfer some of the money from his business account. The bank said that he couldn't. The client was so frustrated he almost gave up. In the end, it was the client's threat to pull all of his money out of the bank that made the bank take another look and approve his line of credit.

I think the most frustrating component to the new financial reality is the lack of common sense. It seems to me that, if Goldman Sachs created a financial debacle and profited from it, they should be shouldering the financial burden, not the American taxpayer. I often feel that if you put one hundred average Americans in a room, by the end of the day, our financial problems would be solved. I think we are seeing a lack of accountability in the financial systems, and it is frustrating to feel unable to do anything to change it.

Before this new financial era, we were at least able to talk to someone at the local level. I can't tell you how many times I am frustrated by the automated answering service my bank now uses exclusively. It seems like it's time to go back to the local credit unions and small banks where there is more personal interaction (and therefore, accountability).

I recently received a debit card with *Rober* printed on it instead of *Robert*. The energy it took to get a correctly printed debit card from my financial institution was unbelievably frustrating. The amount of time and energy it takes to be on top of your investments when the people you are dealing with are apathetic and think that someone else will take care of things is staggering. From overdraft fees to checks being held to just plain bad customer service on the part of banks, it seems like they don't even care if they fail. However, if you try to get a loan at one of these institutions, you would think you were the bad guy.

Turn your frustration around:

- Work on financial flexibility.

- Learn the current financial institution template.

- Support more personal financial institutions (credit unions, small banks, etc.).

Anger

Many people work at jobs they hate and try to suppress their anger. And then they wonder why things never change. Imagine that your workplace was about to begin a new project that encompassed everything that you would like in a job. It would allow you to be creative, have your own free time, and set your own pay scale. Now imagine that your own company was hiring based solely on positive attitude. Would they hire you? Whether you are aware of it or not, this scenario is currently playing out. Even if you are self-employed, the attitude you bring to your work directly affects the outcome of your work.

Anger can work in both positive and negative ways. For some people, anger is a motivator. It can get them out of a slump and give them a new perspective on their situation. Many of us, though, continue to hold on to anger based on past relationships that we cannot change. Our anger only serves to detract from our personal joy and health.

People who say they don't care about money are often the ones who care the most—they just don't have it. There are some people who truly are not money oriented, but most people who make this statement make it out of anger. They are angry that everyone else got the payoff they didn't get. They are mad because they were not given a large inheritance or never got the raise they felt they deserved.

Turn your anger around:

- Cultivate drive and appreciation.

- Be aware that your attitude is reflected in your work.

- Let go of anger.

Become Aware of Your Money Nerve

Through personal experience and over twenty-five years of client interactions, I have become acutely aware of people's Money Nerves. I have seen how a lack of awareness of the emotions that trigger the Money Nerve has wreaked havoc on my clients. Time and time again, I have gotten to the point where I felt I was suggesting a simple, numbers-based decision, but my clients' emotions would surface and take them in a completely different direction.

Herein lies the dilemma: our financial reality is more than just dollars and cents. We are sentient beings governed by a combination of emotions and facts. As is true with all types of emotions, our Money Nerve, when pinched, can also get the best of us. There is no one answer to this dilemma. Emotions are fluid and change over time.

The first day on a new job is an example. You are nervous and worry that you might make a mistake. Three years down the line, you can do your work in your sleep. The things that were important to you when you started the job are not as important now because you have a new set of tools and more information. Your job now is to be aware—as much as possible—of the emotions that rise up when you deal with your finances … and to direct your choices with intention.

Call to Action

Face Your Financial Fears

Answer the following questions in your Money Nerve daily journal.

1. Write down a recent, uncomfortable Money Nerve moment and analyze how you might have mitigated the emotions behind it and improved the situation.

2. Review your journal entries to identify other emotions that trigger your Money Nerve.

3. Make a list of individuals in your inner circle of family and friends with whom you could discuss finances.

4. Make a list of individuals outside of your first circle whom you could ask for financial advice. They might be experts, such as a CPA or a financial advisor, or just someone with whom you would feel comfortable discussing a financial fear.

5. Pick the three most prominent emotions that trigger your Money Nerve and mentally trace them back to what you believe to be the root cause. For example, "My father got angry whenever we wanted to eat out."

6. Continue to journal daily and explore your emotions when processing this information.

3

Come to Terms with Your Money Nerve

Identify Your Fears

NOW THAT YOU ARE BECOMING MORE AWARE of the emotions that trigger your Money Nerve, it's time to address the major roadblock on your path to financial health: fear. Throughout the course of my career, I have noticed trends that blocked my clients' financial progress. As I evaluated these tendencies, I realized that all of them stemmed from fear.

People respond to fear in different ways, and the results almost invariably keep them from moving freely toward their financial goals. In order to come to terms with your Money Nerve, you will need to face your fears.

Sometimes, the story we tell about ourselves doesn't match the reality of who we are. I used to tell myself I was meek and dismissive—certainly not a leader. So I was completely stunned when I won a leadership award at a seminar I attended. At the beginning of that seminar, I never would have claimed to be a leader.

Without our knowledge, the organizers taped our group sessions so we could see ourselves unedited. There, on the television in front of me, was evidence of me offering ideas, leading discussions, and taking control. Maybe I had been acting as a leader for a number of years before I saw myself, but it took being secretly videotaped for me to recognize it. Perhaps I was afraid to step up and claim authority—after all, people might not approve of me or my leadership style. Similarly, you may recognize the story you tell yourself about how you deal with money doesn't match your financial reality.

This chapter is about self-knowledge. By becoming aware of fears that may be roadblocks for you, you will begin to understand what your strengths and weaknesses are (and learn to leverage them to your advantage). You can recognize what connects your Money Nerve at a fundamental level to your financial decision making. This is an integral part of the process of becoming more aware of who you are, financially speaking.

Afraid of the IRS

It's amazing how many people are terrified of the IRS. They view it as the ultimate parent or authority figure. Even when they know they'll get a refund, the process of getting their financial numbers together (and the fear of a possible audit) are enough to make some people avoid dealing with their taxes altogether. If they've avoided filing taxes for years, some believe they'll end up in prison. Debtor prison ended a long time ago. Fines for filing taxes late are real, though. Ignoring tax responsibilities does not make them go away.

When you fear authority and do not take responsibility for your finances, you essentially put the responsibility on others to make decisions. If you're not taking action out of rebellion, you're saying, "I don't like your ideas, so go ahead and do whatever you want." If you're relinquishing your financial responsibilities because of insecurity, you might say, "I'm afraid of doing it wrong, so I will do nothing." It's the same result, different intention.

Sam came to me one day to talk about his taxes. He said, "Um, I don't want anybody to know this, but I haven't filed my taxes in ten years." He was very embarrassed. I completed his returns, and it turned out he had lost all the money due to him in tax refunds because the time the IRS allowed for him to receive a refund had passed. There is no timeframe if you owe the IRS money. Once Sam became current with his filings, he was relieved and promised he would never let it happen again. The next year, I called him to remind him to send me his tax information ... and the next year and the next. I finally stopped calling him. Sam was literally paying the IRS 5,000 dollars per year to not file! It is truly amazing how expensive inaction can be—and inaction is often triggered by fear.

Afraid to Confront

You can be a financial victim out of fear of confronting experts. I know a number of people who have been taken advantage of by their mechanic, their plumber, or their boss. A client was buying a house, and the first piece of advice I gave her was to have a third party—unrelated to the sale—inspect the house. Instead, she had the realtor's friend inspect the house. A couple of weeks after she bought the house, she called me. On the day of final inspection, the owner had incense burning and waterfall music playing throughout the house. It turns out that the smell from the incense was covering up cat urine that had leaked through the floorboards, and the soothing sounds of the waterfall masked a loudspeaker from a carwash near her backyard. When she tried to contact the owner, the owner had already collected all of the money and moved to Europe with no forwarding address.

Some months later, the same client called me and was very upset. She ran out of money to finish remodeling her new house. Knowing her finances at the time, I thought it was a little odd that she had already burned through her remodeling fund. She had been swindled again! Her landscaper told her that the total bill for landscaping her yard would be around 50,000 dollars. She simply agreed and wrote him a check for the entire amount. He was never heard from again.

The common denominator is that financial victims fail to ask the right questions. They fear people will think they are stupid or weak. The remedy could be as simple as one question. In order to avoid being embarrassed, I usually preface my questions in the following way: "Sorry if I'm a little uninformed, but my experience has been that I have to ask questions in order to feel better about this." I actually use the victim in me to help myself. I want to ensure that all of my questions get answered before I complete a transaction. What are the fees involved in this? What does this specifically cover or not cover? How long have you been doing this?

People who want to avoid confrontation look for the easiest way to handle finances. It is a double-edged sword. They are not willing to confront, and yet, by avoiding confrontation, they potentially make the situation worse and even more difficult to confront. The fact that you are putting your head in the sand doesn't mean that your behind is not exposed.

Most people tell me they avoid confronting their finances because they are overwhelmed by the constant nature of financial responsibility. Finances are not something that you can learn one time and forget about. As your life changes (and the economy changes), you have to readjust and relearn. It's similar to driving: you can set a course for your destination, but *you* will have to decide when to exit for fuel or take an alternative route if the road is blocked. You are in the driver's seat.

You may be someone who wants to get something done and quickly move past it. Finances will always be a part of your life—not something you can ever move past. Confront your financial fears and set aside an hour per week to update your records. If you use computer software, input your bank statement and expenses. Balance your checkbook.

Every three months or so, you can sit down and adjust your budget. Make an effort to spend responsibly. Make a list of all bills you get each month, and then check them off your list as you pay them. That way, if you didn't receive a bill, you still realize it has to be paid. Spreadsheets are a great way to keep track of expenditures. Once a year, list your assets and debts to get a sense of your net worth.

If you are willing to be an active participant, you can do more to turn your financial situation around. Start acting like a specialist in your financial life. Get a book like *Investing for Dummies.*[6] No one knows you as well as you know yourself. Accordingly, you are the only one who will be able to make the right financial decision based on what your needs are. People who give away their power to someone else can learn to stand up for themselves. With a little education, you will be able to ask the right questions in the areas that you have yet to understand, which will equip you with all the answers you need.

Write a response to these questions:

Who is making financial decisions for me when I don't make them for myself?

Why is someone else better equipped to make *my* financial decisions?

I used to play an improv game at ACME Comedy Theater called expert. There were two or three improvisers on stage, and the audience would come up with the most outlandish questions possible. The questions were chosen at random, and the improvisers had to assume that they were experts in the chosen field and give responses to the questions. The key was—and is—confidence.

---

6   Eric Tyson, *Investing for Dummies.* 5th ed. (Hoboken: Wiley Publishing, Inc.), 2008.

If it is confidence that you lack, start slowly by educating yourself in a financial area of interest. Try a seminar on funding your retirement, consult with a financial planner (or two) to get advice about directions for college funding, or choose a book on mutual funds and become your own personal financial expert.

Afraid to Picture Possibilities

A number of years ago, a friend of mine asked me to go to Greece and run the original marathon course. I immediately said no because my mental map told me that only rich people traveled, and I was not rich. He finally persuaded me after telling me for months how amazing the experience would be. The marathon was truly everything he said it would be and more.

I remember running past the tomb of Socrates and Plato with Greek citizens cheering me on and offering me grapes. Finally, I could see the marathon finish line inside the first modern Olympic stadium. There, waiting for me, was a group of about a dozen Americans who had already finished. As I crossed the finish line, a wave of emotion came over me. One of the Americans came and touched my shoulder to ask how I was. I could not speak. About half a second later, I fell to the ground and sobbed for several minutes. I had no idea that so much emotion would arise.

Running the marathon made me realize that I was not limited to what people told me was possible or not possible. I almost missed an amazing, life-changing experience by hesitating to say yes. My reaction for months (prior to agreeing to go) was to say no to an opportunity that turned out to be a pivotal moment in my life.

Some people tend to automatically respond to new financial possibilities by saying no. Their response has little to do with whether or not the financial situation is good or bad. It has simply become an automatic response. No is sometimes the appropriate answer. It is the "no!" mindset that should be examined.

A person who is afraid to picture possibilities on a personal level may say things such as, "I can watch TV instead of living my dream," or, "I can take this mediocre job that is not challenging because I'm still getting paid." They still want to climb up the ladder; they just don't want to climb too high. They are afraid of the heights to which they can ascend, so they simply lower their expectations.

Afraid to Part with Money

Saving is very important. Taken to an extreme, however, even saving can be harmful. An extreme saver risks living for a future that never comes. Many people who lived through the Depression and World War II have had difficulty getting past the fear of scarcity. I know people who have paid off their houses completely, yet they never travel or go out to eat. They refuse to buy anything that is not a necessity because they fear that, at any moment, they will be thrown into the streets. Their whole lives can pass them by because they live in fear of a possible future financial event.

My friend visited his grandmother in Poland. She had lived through terrible times. While there, he got into a big argument with his grandmother after he took it upon himself to clean out her refrigerator. He was about to throw out rotten meat when his grandmother stopped him and started yelling at him. The meat was green and clearly rotten, yet she was so upset that she began crying. She was still guided by a mental map that said she could be without access to food at any moment. She had seen people die of starvation during her life, and even though circumstances had changed in Poland, she continued to live in the past.

There is nothing wrong with putting away a three-month supply of food so that you are covered in case of an emergency. I just don't recommend sacrificing your present life for an unforeseeable future.

Right now, as I write this book, I am hiking through the Himalayas. This is the second time I have hiked the Himalayas, and it has taken me years to find the time. It is never convenient or easy to do. I think of my friend's grandmother finding an envelope labeled *Hawaii trip* in her husband's safe deposit box after he died. They never left mainland soil in his lifetime. He had plenty of money in the envelope; he just waited too long to take action.

Sometimes, one spouse finds financial freedom when the other dies. Jack and Sally grew up during the Depression, and although they were financially stable in their retirement, they rarely vacationed and never remodeled their aging house. After Sally's passing, Jack found new financial freedom. He bought a new truck, he remodeled his house, and he sends a holiday letter each year describing his incredible travel adventures. Sally's financial fears kept both of them from sharing special experiences.

Savers who regularly deny themselves life's pleasures typically come from a generation that has experienced hardship. Current American culture, on the other hand, teaches that all needs can be met with a credit card. We live for the moment—not only neglecting to think about the future, but also sacrificing future stability for instant gratification. It is important to find a balance between saving and spending.

Afraid to Be Judged

Fear of what others may think is a major contributor to denial. Some people make negative judgments about others' financial choices, and then they find it difficult to be honest when budgeting their own finances. When you sit down to create your budget, your list of expenses might exclude things that don't "look good," or things that you wish were not true. However, this is not just about alcohol, cigarettes, or other vices. You may be reluctant to put down something that others view as a positive, such as a spa day or a gym membership.

About five years ago, one of my clients, a physician, started to show large increases of cash coming in. I kept seeing cash increases of ten thousand here and five thousand there, so I had to ask where the money was coming from. He was a doctor who administered Botox, and many of his clients paid in cash because they didn't want anyone to know they had the procedure. Not only are people afraid of being judged as old or imperfect, they are afraid of being judged for their insecurities that lead them to alter their looks.

People justify their situation to others in different ways to avoid being judged. I used to work with an extremely religious client who invested in 976 sex talk numbers. She was making about 300,000 dollars per year by owning four machines with women's recordings. Every time she met with me, she said she had to sell her business because it was immoral and wrong for people to be calling. When I suggested she could easily stop the business, she immediately began to justify holding onto it. She talked about how the money was going to good use, and she said that she was donating to the church, which she really did not do. Remember, it is hard to lie to your accountant. In her mind, as long as she didn't add any additional phone lines, she was doing the right thing. But she certainly never told her congregation about her business.

Justifying lifestyle choices may seem harmless until they catch up with you. Just as ignoring regular maintenance on your car because you don't want to spend the money that week can result in major car expenses down the line, poor spending or saving habits may also result in a later retirement and fewer choices down the road. What is important is to recognize that you are justifying. Once you've acknowledged that, you can then determine whether it is good or bad for you. The moment you recognize the justification in your finances, you should go back to the basics. Take a look at your budgeting and stop making excuses for your financial position.

Afraid to Lose Control

At a recent seminar, many of the attendees stated that they were proud of being control freaks. I had always thought being a control freak was negative. And yet, the people attending the conference were proud of that personality trait. The seminar theme was getting specific about our goals. What I took from the event was this: if we are specific in defining our goals, our life will be specific. When you have a clear picture of what you want in your mind, you have a greater chance of manifesting it.

Fear can lead to a desire to control virtually everything. Controllers may feel there is only one way to do things: their way. Financial controllers shrink life down to something that is manageable for them. This means that they are also narrowing their possibilities. If you have a controlling person in your life, you may be experiencing the by-product. Your boss might be controlling because he or she is unable to handle certain personal affairs. Life at home might be so out of control that your boss micromanages every little detail at work.

Let's face it: we cannot handle everything all the time. There may be things that happened to us in the past that we had no control over (and that continue to play a role in our daily decision making). People who are afraid to lose control tend to break down scenarios into the most simplistic version and then dominate that simplicity. They may feel empowered, but they are ultimately doing themselves a disservice by creating a smaller version of a full life.

Afraid to Challenge Belief Systems

When I was in Toastmasters, I gave a speech on an American hero. The hero I picked was a college basketball player who was protesting the war in Iraq. At every basketball game, she turned her back to the American flag while the "Star Spangled Banner" was played. My choice upset a lot of people. At the end of my speech, I said the reason I chose that young lady as an American hero was because she was brave enough to exercise her right to freedom of expression. I quoted a number of military personnel who said they would fight to the death for her right to turn her back on the flag.

A few weeks later, the Toastmasters's president approached me to tell me how upset my speech had made her initially. She could not believe I dared to choose that woman. She said that the interesting part was that, after she thought about it for a while, she realized my speech had shifted her belief system. I had created the opportunity for her to take a look at all of the factors in the story, including our first amendment rights.

Morals are a great barometer, and it's important not to be blindsided by those morals. Be willing to hear other options. Using your money to force others to do what you think is the best choice may serve you in the short run, but ultimately such action does a disservice to everyone. Financing medical school but not vocational school for your grandchildren (because your family is made up of doctors) is a good example of this phenomenon. One client paid for his son's car and covered his rent because he was the "good" son. His daughter did not adhere to the family's expectations and was financially excluded.

It is sometimes easier to live within a set of rules that defines you. It is hard to stand out by yourself. When the Dixie Chicks first came out against the war in Iraq, even their die-hard fans lashed out against them. Radio stations stopped playing their songs, and concerts had to be canceled. History ultimately proved the Dixie Chicks had a valid point, but people generally aren't comfortable with taking a stand against the majority opinion. A moralist loves black and white, it is more comfortable—which is why I like lots of gray! I am not saying you should live your life without morals, though—I think extremes of any kind can be dangerous.

If your automatic response to any new idea is to reject it, start cultivating a more accepting and positive point of view. Oftentimes, if your automatic answer is no, you will miss out on whatever is waiting to be revealed to you (financially or otherwise).

It is very much a catch-22 situation: the more you deny possibilities, the more likely you will become frustrated. Your inner monologue will never change unless you start to allow yourself to say yes to new ideas.

Instead of confrontation, practice understanding and openness so you can see that there is more than one way.

Afraid of Being Unworthy

Generally speaking, we all want to believe we are special. We want to believe that there is a reason for our existence. Some people are people pleasers because they do not believe they are as special as they would like to be. Sometimes, the desire to be liked is so strong that they become lost in a never-ending pursuit of approval. A problem may exist when the need for approval is stronger than a person's intentions. Financial decisions are much easier to make with a strong, specific intention in mind.

Sometimes, people overcompensate to prove they are worthy. Driven by insecurity, they try to make up for the fact that they think they're inadequate. Many are trying to prove something; they have a mindset that might say, *I'm envious that you have a degree, so I'm going to overcompensate by showing you how much gold I have.*

I often witness this feeling surface in conversations with people whom others would view as extremely successful. I am shocked by the number of people who make good money but do not feel worthy—they are just waiting for someone to discover they are undeserving. Some actors, artists, and businesspeople who make it big feel like they got a break they didn't deserve when they compare themselves to friends in the same field. Some compare themselves to family or friends who are even wealthier (thus making them feel unworthy). It's not reality—and it's the way they feel. We're taught that if it came easily, it's not real; we have to suffer in some way for it to be real.

I was sitting in a stopped car in high school when I was rammed from behind by another car. I was so afraid to confront the driver that I didn't say anything and just drove away (even though I was not at fault). I was paralyzed because I didn't recognize my own value. In the end, I felt far worse for not having spoken up—there were dents not only in my car and pocketbook, but also in my self-esteem. Feeling financially unworthy means that you feel like you don't deserve to be wealthy. It keeps you from attaining your definition of real financial success. The financially unworthy have a difficult time envisioning themselves with a satisfactory amount of money.

Afraid to Face the Truth

To try to prove they are good enough, some people tell financial lies. The most damaging lies are the ones that you tell yourself. Have you ever heard someone say, "Everything is fine; I can handle it," while breaking down in tears? In Los Angeles, many people have built an image of themselves based on material possessions. Such an image is a giant house of cards just waiting for the smallest disturbance to knock it down. I have many clients who come into my office and say, "If anyone knew my real situation, I would be devastated."

Pop culture and advertising are the biggest catalysts for creating a financial lie. *You are not good enough. You are not skinny enough. You are not rich enough.* These are some of the constructs that advertising tries to sell us in order to create a feeling of insecurity. Advertisers would like us to think that purchasing their products is the only way to alleviate our problems.

In a way, credit cards are a financial lie. If you say that you can afford something because you were able to charge it on a credit card, you are not being totally truthful because you just created a debt. A lie is the intentional opposition of the truth, and it is easy to lie to ourselves every day. Alcoholics routinely say, "I am never going to drink again." Yet many return to the bottle the next day. If you are constantly lying to yourself, you are living a false life.

Afraid to Stop Enabling

I know many parents who enable their children to the point that their children never grow up. The children expect a certain type of lifestyle. I have yet to meet anyone who respects the things that they did not have to earn. I continue to categorize them as children because a consequence of having been enabled is that you never have to grow up and take responsibility.

Enabling does not empower; enabling tends to stunt growth. You cannot move forward because you have not been taught to seek out new information you may need to improve your position. Why would you? Enabling is almost always done with the best of intentions, but ultimately, it does not produce the best results.

How does this affect your finances? I have had clients who confide that their spouses are spending beyond their paycheck, and they still refuse to confront the issue. Almost every day, I hear about relationships that have problems revolving around money issues. The healthy relationships tend to be the ones that deal with the Money Nerve on a regular basis.

Many people justify being a workaholic because doing so allows their family to have the best of everything. However, many times, all the family wants is to have more time with them. Some parents work incredibly hard to establish a lifestyle that requires other people to take care of their kids.

A good friend of mine only saw his parents on Sunday for dinner. He was raised in boarding schools. His parents thought they were doing the right thing for his future, but my friend felt unwanted. It makes sense to want to provide for your children, and it's important to factor in other components besides money.

My belief is that an interpersonal relationship is more important than a monetary relationship. I have friends who don't have a lot of money and have amazing relationships with their children. I think that is the healthier choice. Ideally, one could have both.

Who doesn't like to be taken care of? Financial enablers often see themselves as caregivers and unwittingly create a needy person. I know people who pay their kids' bills and take care of the grandchildren. Their kids, in turn, have basically stopped parenting. The grandparents are the ones who attend parent-teacher conferences and ballgames. The grandparents have become the parents, and they don't necessarily find it to be so grand.

Most of the time, people who are being taken care of do not take advantage of opportunities. If you are making life easy for someone, they tend to take it easy. Caregivers unwillingly support a lack of growth and a lack of effort on the part of the individual being financially enabled.

Afraid to Fix the Cause

The financial quick-fixer has a duct tape mentality, and contrary to popular belief, duct tape doesn't fix everything. You may get immediate results, but you are not actually dealing with the cause of the problem. If you are overdrawn in your bank account, you might think you are doing right by using your credit card to bring your account back into balance. That is robbing Peter to pay Paul. The reality is that you are creating more debt for yourself *and* adding interest payments to what you owe already.

I joke that I wish I could "un-know" what I know. It is a lot more work when you start to take responsibility for your life. Imagine going to a seminar and hearing that there are eight steps you have to take in order to become a millionaire. Many people in the seminar will stop at four steps. Some people will even say, "I've finished four steps, why don't I have 500,000 dollars?"

We live in a volatile world. Financial quick-fixers sometimes thrive on being able to solve the small problems around them. Often, these are the exact same problems they have created. Like an addict, quick-fixers enjoy the immediate boost of self-confidence they receive from solving an issue. If you spend a lot of time in the quick-fix mentality, you may actually like being there.

Address Your Fears

Addressing your fears is all about perspective. Recognizing your financial fears will enable you to begin to face them. When you put your fears aside, you open up new ways of seeing. You may find more value in yourself, your relationships, and your financial future.

I used to be a consistent runner. I ran cross-country, and I have been fortunate to run a few marathons. There is a process to running long distances. You can't just wake up and decide to run twenty-six miles. You start with one mile and do that for several weeks to slowly build up your stamina. Your first financial mile involves starting to educate yourself about your budget and what you want to accomplish. And then you must make a plan. If one of the above fears applies to you, you need to plan your way out of it. Start slowly and make sure you track your progress. If you do not track it, you will not believe you are succeeding.

Many of the people who have these fears are not taking responsibility. The reason I like running is because I can only blame myself for my performance. I race myself. Nobody else can tell me to get up in the morning to run. Your financial health is a long-distance run. There will be people along the way to help you—financial advisors, CPAs, and others will assist you and put you on the right path, however you are the one running the race. They give you support, but at the end of the day, it is your money.

Your finances are going to be there tomorrow, next weekend, on your vacation, and even on your birthday. Facing your finances is the first step. There is no physical harm in facing your financial reality. No one has ever been stabbed by a bank account. You may feel a pang in your stomach, and you are fine. Acknowledging your financial situation and taking steps to confront it is a good start.

Find a champion in your life for every area that you fear. If you are afraid of not having enough money for retirement, you should find someone who has worked with retirement planning and thinks of it as second nature. Don't limit your champions to your friends. You can go outside your inner circle and find someone at work. Alternatively, you can read books, articles, and websites on the subject. Start with the easiest fear to overcome and become educated in that area of financial fear. With education and support, you can face your fears one at a time, come to terms with your Money Nerve, and start to move forward.

Call to Action

Identify Fears That Affect Your Finances

Answer the following questions in your Money Nerve daily journal.

1. Make a list of your top five financial fears.

2. Next, describe specifically how these fears may affect your finances.

3. Describe how these fears may affect the key financial relationships in your life (e.g., those with your spouse, siblings, parents, or children).

4. Go back to the first question in this exercise and write the name of a financial champion next to each financial fear.

5. Write down a plan to help you address your easiest fear. How can your financial champion be a resource for you?

6. Keep writing in your daily journal.

4

Assess Your Budget

A Reality Check

THIS CHAPTER IS A REALITY CHECK. WHERE are you *really?* You can't get to your ultimate destination if you don't know your starting point. In this chapter, we will look at income and expense budgeting, time budgeting, and hidden costs. When you do these things, it is really important to be honest with yourself. What do you *really* earn? What do you *really* spend? What do you pretend is not relevant to your budget?

This chapter is important to me because this area is where I see the most self-deception. Most people round up on their income and round down on their expenses. If you really want to get ahead and really want to be honest, *always* lower your income estimates and raise your expense estimates. This will help give you a cushion for the realities of your inflows and outflows of cash.

This process will be painful for many people. When I address budget assessment with most clients, they want to bolt. This could get ugly. We need the truth, the whole truth, and nothing but the truth.

Income

Positive Flow

Budgeting is often considered from an *expenses* point of view (income is simply viewed as a fixed component). Few people take the time to analyze all the areas that provide income. It is important to become aware of the flow of money coming in and going out.

Many of my clients tend to think that the only way to improve their monthly budgeting is to cut costs (for example, sharing office space to decrease rent or ride sharing to decrease commuting costs). Cutting down expenses is certainly important, and increasing revenue is equally as important. People forget about asking for a raise, looking for better employment, or taking on a second job.

One way to improve your budget is to cut away whatever ideas might be holding you back from increasing your income. Be open to the possibility that you might have ways to increase your cash intake.

For instance, here are some ideas that block financial success:

- Self-doubt.

- Working from home is not seen as professional.

- Marketing to friends may hurt relationships.

- Working weekends is not an option (if your job requires flexibility).

- Working weekends is the only way to make it financially.

- Assuming your business doesn't qualify for a loan or grant or internship—so failing to apply for one.

After you address your financial blocks, you can also consider positive ways to augment your income sources, which ultimately benefits your budgeting. You might spend more time networking or make yourself more available to opportunities by keeping your cell phone on all the time.

Know Your Value

A great way to start looking for ways to augment your income is to research what people are making in your field. Find out what other people are getting paid and how much work they produce. Then ask yourself, *Do I do all that is possible in my position to demonstrate my value?*

One of my clients is an engineer. She does all the programming and reviews, and she writes troubleshooting software at her firm. She spent years at another firm training men and watching them get promoted to higher-level, more lucrative positions. Frustrated, she initiated talks with her present company. They immediately agreed to hire her for 100,000 dollars—about double what she was making at the time.

She was excited until she realized that the men at her new job (who had less experience) were still making more than her. This upset her. She met with her new boss and said, "I love it here, and I'm excited, but knowing that my colleagues with less experience are making more money makes me feel cheated. I am trying to figure out how to reconcile that." Her boss immediately gave her a 30,000 dollar raise.

Sometimes, you aren't earning what you think you should earn. But have you asked for more? Maybe you know your value and are afraid to ask to be compensated for it. There are people who sit in jobs for years and years and don't ask for a raise. If you don't ask for it, you may never receive it. Initiative is often rewarded.

Sit down and make a list of all the value you add to your job. Arrange a meeting with your boss, produce your list, and say: "It's been two years since my last raise, and I feel I have earned another one. I always take care of the things I've listed here. I've helped guide you through some critical junctures and kept things flowing. I feel like I am worth it."

Time Budgeting

Budgeting is also about time management. Sometimes, you don't factor in all of your time for a given business project. Also, work might affect your personal time—you might not budget time for yourself or your children's activities, for instance.

Schedule out your day with time frames and ask yourself if you can really accomplish all of the tasks in a day. Maybe yes, maybe no. Either way, it's about discipline and figuring out what you personally can do in a day (not what your friend or sister or dad can do). Don't compare yourself to others. Focus on *you*.

Looking at my time budgeting actually improved my billing revenue. I hired an independent consultant to evaluate my company. I invested about 3,000 dollars to have him grade my staff's performance (as well as my own). Although I received high marks for customer service and employee satisfaction, he noted my billing was below the industry standard. I knew that I could complete corporate tax returns more quickly than other accountants, but I wasn't factoring my productivity level into my billing. The consultant helped me realize that my time was more valuable per hour than that of someone who worked more slowly.

Having more information about how other firms worked and what they provided gave me more confidence to bill what I was worth. I receive more income than before, which gives me more choices. I can decide to work less, maintain my income, and create more family time—or I may choose to work more and have an even higher level of income. Either way, by knowing my value, I have more control over how I choose to live my life.

Honest Assessment

While working on a self-employed client's tax return, he reviewed it and told me I had made a critical error. I reported that he earned 250,000 dollars in gross receipts. He said that was impossible. He thought he only earned about half of that. I told him it was possible I made a mistake, and I offered to review the details with him.

I told him that he earned so much from one company, and so much from another. One by one, he told me, "Yes, I earned that. Yes, I earned that, too." And then I said, "Well if you did in fact earn all of those individually, they total up to 250,000 dollars. You really did earn that." He was astounded. "I can't believe I really earned all of that. It seems to go so fast." The point is, he did earn the money—he just didn't know where it went. The next part of this chapter deals with budgeting outflows.

Now we are ready to take an action. We are going to look at your personal cash inflows. That's the money coming to you each week, each month, each year. Looking at these figures and making an honest assessment is the only way to get an accurate representation of your situation. You are going to make a list of all the money coming in and going out. Every dime in—every penny you find on the ground—and every cent you spend (including the secret candy bar and other items you pretend you don't pay for).

Without knowing the full circumstances of your current situation, you can't begin to change it. It is time to take control of your life and get off the financial autopilot you have been on. When you start your list for the week, write at the top by hand:

"I am going to list all my money, in and out, for the week of October 1st through October 7th. I will be completely honest and without judgment."

What Is Your Income?

Start with the money you earn. If you make 52,000 dollars per year, what does that really mean? If you get a paycheck, go get it and look at the net number. Multiply that by fifty-two (if paid weekly), twenty-six (if paid every two weeks), or twenty-four (if paid bi-monthly). Divide your result by twelve to come up with your monthly net income. That's what you take home. You can't budget based on 1,000 dollars per week if your after-tax income is closer to 750 dollars.

Once you know your monthly income, take into account any other money that comes in. If you get a commission check, count it. If your grandma still gives you twenty dollars for your birthday, count it. You have to count it all.

Money Coming to Me

Consider duplicating this list in your daily journal if you prefer to keep your personal information private.

Paycheck (or unemployment or disability) _____

Rent money from roommate _____

Gifts (birthday money, e.g.) _____

Inheritance _____

Social security _____

Parental support _____

Loan repayments from family or friends _____

Lottery _____

Any surprises on your income list? Just what you expected? Either way, make a note of it in your head. You are bringing your finances to your consciousness. You are taking action.

Outflow

Hidden Costs

A friend of mine had trouble budgeting. Sometimes she, like many of us, didn't think about additional or hidden costs. She had trouble seeing the big picture. She could handle what was in front of her, but she was overwhelmed by what she didn't see. She was constantly short of money because she had forgotten about this cost or that cost. She once forgot she was supposed to pay the mortgage and bought Christmas presents instead.

To help her get more realistic about her budgeting, her daughter taught her how to manage her cash flow. All of her incoming money was deposited into a bank account that my friend agreed not to access. Her daughter gave her a weekly stipend that was put into different envelopes labeled *mortgage, food, auto, phone,* and *miscellaneous.* If my friend spent all of her food money, she would be forced to pull money from another envelope. Regardless of how she spent it, those envelopes would not be replenished until the following week. She had to start making choices—and she realized that her funds were limited.

Now she has learned to live within her means. She knows if she wants to buy arts and craft supplies or see a play, she has to choose to reduce her spending in another category. This can be an excellent exercise to help you see the real-time effects of your spending habits.

Hidden costs are expenses that are not normally included in a purchase and may affect you in the future. Smoking is a good example. You may think it's just five bucks right now, and you're not including the hidden cost of health bills down the road. You should ask yourself what the total cost is—the real cost—rather than simply look at what you are paying now. Many of us don't think about all of the additional or hidden costs when we make a purchase or investment or win a prize.

My aunt used to win a prize almost every time my uncle put her name in a bowl or bought her a raffle ticket. She won free cruises, groceries, and toys. She even won a new boat. Free. Well, sort of free. She had to pay income taxes on the value of the boat. They had to get boat insurance. They had never owned a boat, so they signed up for boating lessons. The boat needed a trailer. They needed a tow hitch. They loved that free boat, but they spent a lot of money on it.

Ominous hidden costs that are still very relevant today are loan fees. The recent refinancing boom was a bonanza for mortgage brokers. Some lenders added outrageous fees on the back end of the loan. They added a point here and a point there based on their knowledge that people wouldn't notice the fees. It's basically stealing money, with the approval of the borrower, because most people don't read the contracts they are signing. Many people think, "If I don't have to pay for it today, I'm not really paying for it."

I had a client who seemed determined to sabotage his financial success. Every time he started making money and getting new clients, he began the sabotage. At one point, he was driving drunk and got a DUI that ended up costing him over 30,000 dollars. Besides the fine for the DUI, he lost his license and had to take a taxi to work each day for six months. His insurance tripled. He had to take a DUI class, join Alcoholics Anonymous, and pay the lawyer who defended him in court.

The icing on the cake was that, as he was spending the night in jail, he got robbed. Apparently, the tow truck driver was running a scam that entailed notifying his friends whenever the police called him to tow a drunk driver. If you are not aware of the hidden costs of your actions, you might just find yourself with an empty bank account—and an empty house.

Okay, why should you care about the effects of hidden costs? It's important to have that information in the back of your mind as you budget so that you will have a complete picture of where you stand.

Friend and Family Loans

I don't recommend borrowing or lending money from or to friends and family. Choose that option only as a last resort. If you do so, it is important to be very clear about the terms. Treat any borrowing or lending as a business transaction—especially with family and friends who may have a complex history with you that could become ignited if repayment is not forthcoming. If you leave the terms vague, you may be shorting yourself on the payback. I know some folks who borrow back and forth with each other and never clear up who owes what. I also know folks who borrow money and say, "Well, I helped you fix your roof, so now we're even."

Let's say you borrow money from a friend. A few days later, you buy lunch for the person you borrowed from as means of repayment. Now you have confused the issue because he or she may still feel you owe the money. Essentially, you've bought lunch instead of paying interest. I've done this before. Somebody lent me five bucks, so I bought them a twenty-dollar meal to make up for the five bucks. I just spent an extra fifteen bucks. That's 300 percent interest. Sometimes you think you're saving … and you're not. This is another example of a hidden cost factor.

Credit Card Payments and Interest

Often, I ask clients what they're paying in interest on their credit cards, and they don't know. We'll take a look and find they're paying 29 percent. "Geez, I wish I had known," they say. Actually, they had the information every month; they just chose not to regard it as important. I ask my clients to list every credit card they have. They need to note the credit card carrier, the rate, the interest charged (if any), and the balance. When they see "Citibank, 12 percent; Sears, 18 percent," they say, "Wow, this has to change."

Here's the thing: I was there. I did that. I charged whatever I wanted. It was a future debt, not relevant to today. Eventually, I realized that I was in over my head, and I didn't want to have lots of debt because it was holding me back.

Here is what I did: I didn't want to chop up my credit cards, so I put them in a plastic container full of water and froze them. It was great because, if I really needed the credit card, I had to wait for it to thaw. I tell my clients to do the same thing because I really want them to put a *freeze* on their credit cards. Most of the time, if they actually do start to let a card thaw because they need it, they realize by the time it melts that they really don't need it after all.

Self-Employment Taxes

I have many self-employed clients who think that, because taxes aren't automatically taken out of their profits, they don't need to factor them into their budget. Those clients are the ones scrambling when the tax bill comes. Factor taxes in and put the money aside in a separate account to later mail to the government when your taxes come due.

Nobody likes to pay taxes, but we do like having working roads, libraries, buses, medical services, schools, and many other government-provided services. Pay your taxes.

Money Going Out ... Out ... Out of Control

Okay, here's the tough part: looking at your spending habits. Where does the money go? Oh yeah, you are going to write it all down, especially the stuff you don't want to admit to. You are only lying to yourself if you omit anything. Remember: this is not about making moral judgments on how you spend your money; it's about where all of your money really goes.

Try to take the emotion out of this exercise by saying, "Good or bad, I'm going to write down what I spent my money on." Write it down if you buy ten candy bars or pick up five lottery tickets or toss fifty cents into the tip jar at the coffeehouse. Everything. Write it down. You are trying to get honest with yourself. If you don't put down everything, you can't really get a full assessment of where you stand financially. This is getting to know the real you.

I had a client who used to write a list of all his purchases so I could do his taxes at the end of the year. In his spending detail, he included mushrooms, pot, condoms, and paraphernalia. I'm not saying to go out and spend your money on those things—the point is that he was honestly recording where his money went.

If you have some little vice you don't want anyone to know about, list it under *personal* (or some other code word), but factor it in. After seeing it on paper, you may or may not decide to change your habits. In any event, you need to be honest. No one needs to know the details of your spending … except you. If you are worried someone will see your list, use code words. But *write everything down.*

Money Going Out

Consider duplicating this list in your daily journal if you prefer to keep your personal information private.

    Rent or mortgage   _____

    Utilities   _____

    Cable TV   _____

    Groceries   _____

    Coffeehouse   _____

    Restaurants   _____

    Drinks or alcohol   _____

    Education   _____

Recreation or fitness   _____

Entertainment   _____

Medical expenses   _____

Manicure or hair styling or massage   _____

Pet food or supplies   _____

Personal   _____

Auto expenses   _____

Insurance: car or health or life or house   _____

Loan payback   _____

Interest: loans or credit cards   _____

Taxes   _____

Savings   _____

Investments   _____

Weekly lottery tickets   _____

When you record your cash outflows, you need to be aware of the hidden costs touched upon earlier. They shouldn't change your current outflow, but when you start prioritizing later, having this information will be helpful.

Savings

Budget for Your Future

Are you saving? If you are in the hole one hundred dollars this month (and you continue down that path), how long will it be before you get so far behind that you will not be able to turn it around? You need to create a savings habit. Some financial advisors suggest paying off all debt before saving. I believe you should pay off debt and save simultaneously.

Start putting twenty-five dollars into a savings account. Today. Now. Set up an automatic debit with the bank so that, when your paycheck is deposited on the 5th to your checking account, an automatic transfer into your savings account will occur on the 6th. Start this habit at the same time you learn to pay down your debts. You have to learn to do both. Yes, you'll pay a little more interest than if you put the extra twenty-five dollars toward the credit card debt, but you'll start to see your savings account grow. My experience is that, as people start to save a little, they feel a sense of accomplishment and can't wait to start putting more away.

Remind yourself to pay yourself first. That is what saving is about: paying yourself for your future. People say they want to pay themselves first, and they usually don't follow through. I ask my clients, "Why aren't you saving?" I often hear, "I'm waiting because I'm going to get this big check, and then I'm going to kick-start my savings plan." Or they say, "I want to pay off all my debt before I start saving."

However, my experience with many clients (and my previous self) is that we often promise ourselves to save, and we rarely do. There usually is *not* a big windfall or a money tree that lets us clear all our debts and obligations. Assume no big lottery win and start putting away small amounts. Get into the new habit of saving. You should start with twenty-five dollars. Start experiencing the gratification of seeing your savings grow while paying down your credit cards and other debts. Learn the habit of saving while honoring your prior financial obligations.

I empty my change into a jar. I have maybe eighty bucks of change at the end of the year. I have three or four jars. Once one fills up, I add another jar. If you like to save your change in a jar like I do, you don't even have to start another jar. Take the change down to the bank and throw it into your savings account where it will earn a little interest. It may be small change, but lots of small change turns into dollars.

You don't have to be a millionaire to get into the habit of saving. The *Lawrence Daily Journal-World* ran an article about a janitor at a local college.[7] He ended up leaving close to a million dollars to the school. He'd worked for the college for thirty years, audited economics courses, and had conversations with economics professors. He lived frugally, invested wisely, and died with over a million dollars. If he did it, you can do it. It's doable; do it.

Deposit Regularly

Start slowly. Transfer your savings to another bank so that the savings account does not automatically cover an overdraft. Start to log in on a regular basis to verify that you are a person who saves money. Allow the feeling of saving money to become part of who you are. Frequently, people wait until they have a big chunk of money before they start a savings account. The small amounts that you see when you log in to check your account can become a sort of challenge to be improved upon. You may find yourself becoming fixated on savings.

This happened to a good friend of mine. Several years ago, he was living with me and landed his first job. I helped him set up a savings plan to put aside 300 dollars per month. He had very few expenses at the time. He followed the savings plan every month without fail. As a side benefit, he started to live a healthier lifestyle (the money he was saving was money he would normally spend at a bar).

He loved checking his account and seeing the amounts go up and up. He eventually increased the amount he was saving per month and paid cash for a new car. He began to ask himself how he could live on less

---

7   "Janitor / Stock Expert Leaves Money to School," *The Lawrence Daily Journal-World,* April 19, 1988, Lawrence, Kansas, Vol. 130, No. 110, p.1.

so he could save even more. After about five years, he saved enough to make a down payment on a house.

He was someone who needed guidance. He was great at following a schedule, and I was able to set him up with a plan. As you improve your choices and become someone who is comfortable with money and consistent with your savings, you will be able to help others do the same. You can shift from being someone who needs financial help to someone who gives help.

Emergency Fund

You also need an emergency fund. I am not talking about the emergency kit that we should all have in our homes (containing water, canned food, and a little radio, e.g.). Though emergency resources often include physical supplies such as blankets and bandages, they should also include emergency funds.

You should keep a credit card clear for emergencies. Put a credit card with a zero balance in a drawer, and only use it enough to keep the credit card valid (many credit card companies now close accounts with no activity). This method usually entails making a purchase with the card and paying it back quickly to avoid interest. This card is for emergencies—real emergencies.

When Katrina hit, it took people two or three months to receive FEMA credit cards. There were people who actually went without food for weeks. Most of them did not have access to available credit. If you don't have an emergency kit, buy a few items at a time and stock up ... and include a credit card.

You should also have cash put aside for your emergency fund. There are unforeseen circumstances that occur in all of our lives, and we need to be prepared to handle them. Being laid off or not being able to work would qualify as an emergency. Start budgeting so that you can build that emergency fund.

I don't expect you to arrive at your destination tomorrow, and the time to start is now. An ideal emergency fund would cover six months of your current monthly expenses. You are on the road to financial health when you take this step to prepare for your future.

Other Budget Considerations

Cost-Benefit Analysis

Most people are familiar with the following phrase: "What's in it for me?" Cost-benefit analysis is the process of weighing the total expected costs against the total expected benefits of your actions in order to choose the most beneficial option. It is important to express all benefits and costs in monetary terms.

You're going to have to budget to see this. For example, you may say, "I really need a vacation to Hawaii now. It's going to help me relax and feel less stressed. If I charge a package trip to Hawaii now, I'm willing to give up my weekly massage and put 200 dollars per month toward my credit card until my credit card is paid off." There are no physical reminders, so you need to be disciplined and follow through with your budgeting choices.

Budget for Health

Healthcare is so expensive it is almost prohibitive. I recognize health insurance is a hot button issue, and the costs are out of control. A portion of budgeting should take into account how important health is to financial well-being. Are you budgeting for beer, soda, and fattening foods rather than making time available for exercise? Are you paying for your own health problems?

I have a personal trainer whom I pay to come to my house three times per week to lead me in a workout. Some people say this is an unnecessary expense. For me, it is worth it to pay a trainer to help keep me in shape and keep my diet on track. I am a much happier and healthier human being when I am consistent with my workouts.

I factor the trainer into my budget by looking for trade-offs. I pay twenty dollars per month for basic cable instead of paying for premium channels because I don't watch much television. I feel that watching television is not something that contributes to my overall well-being. I have chosen a different priority. There are many ways to prioritize your expenses that will serve you in a healthy way.

How Not to Budget

Danny and his wife came to me because they were struggling to pay their bills. They had maxed out credit cards. They had car payments with an average of 20 percent in interest. I took a look at their finances and saw they were able to qualify for a 100,000 dollar equity line of credit on their house. I showed them how they could take out a loan, consolidate all the credit card and auto loan debts, and get a tax break.

I saw them twelve months later and asked how they were doing. "Terrible," Danny said. He told me that he had all sorts of emergencies and had to use all of his credit cards again. He maxed out every single credit card on top of the equity loan.

If I had known they were not disciplined enough to follow the plan, I would never have told them they qualified for a home equity line of credit. He took what would have been a great plan and pretended his new credit card zero balances were newly found money. Everything became an emergency, and he doubled his debt. Getting a forty-two-inch plasma TV is *not* an emergency, no matter how much you enjoy it.

Ignoring income is not a good way to budget, either. I assisted a friend of a friend with an audit. I don't always make good decisions! She was sure that the IRS was wrong, that she did not owe additional taxes. When I looked at her deposits, I realized that there was about 30,000 dollars she had not claimed on her return. I asked her about the money, and she said that she did not count that money because it was paid to her in cash for her side jobs. She also mentioned that, because her life goal wasn't to be a waitress, she didn't count her tips. I said that the IRS didn't care how she saw herself.

If you earn the money, the IRS wants its cut. She wasn't being realistic about her income. Had she been more realistic about her income, she may have been more aware of her expenses ... including paying taxes.

Finding the Balance

Work your desires into your budget. If I don't have enough money for a purchase, I don't buy it. I had been saving up for a television and decided that I was going to spend between 1,000 and 1,500 dollars for one. I went to the store with my sister (she is an electronics super genius). I asked her which television I should get. She talked about switching to HD and other options, and I was having a hard time deciding. I wanted to get the right one.

Suddenly, a young couple walked up and looked around until the husband said, "Honey, look! They've got flat screen televisions. If we buy one today, it's only 3,500 dollars—we'd save 1,500 dollars." So they went to the checkout counter and charged it to their credit card just like that. I heard their entire conversation while they were looking around. It was an impulse buy. How does someone just walk into a store and spend 3,500 dollars because they're so excited that they'll save 1,500 dollars? Impulsive financial decisions may have long-term financial effects.

Find a compromise. It doesn't have to be all or nothing. It reminds me of one of my clients who complained she never had any money. After looking at her expenses, I noticed that, every Wednesday, she spent a lot of money at different bars and restaurants. She referred to it as her "obligatory girl's night out." I didn't tell her she shouldn't go out and drink with her friends. I just suggested she have a drink at home first or eat a little bit before going out.

The group started meeting at one another's house before going out. They sat around, chatted, and had a glass of wine before hitting the bars. Eventually, they skipped out on the bar scene completely. Now, they pool their money and have amazing catered dinners at home. They are much happier and still save money.

Revise Your Spending

Once you know where your money comes from and where it goes, you can take steps to change the flow if needed. You may find that your current spending habits keep you from getting ahead. It took me a year to eliminate a kickboxing gym membership. I wanted to be able to kick butt, but the fees were the only thing kicking butt. I didn't even have time to go to the classes. I held on to the membership because I wanted to envision myself as an active kickboxer. I spent over a hundred dollars per month to pretend I was Jean Claude Van Damme. The only weight some people lose by having a gym membership is the money weight they lose from their wallet each month.

Now that you are aware of your Money Nerve, you can begin to assess which expenses *really* serve to feed your financial growth—and which expenses *really* starve your financial future.

Call to Action

Assess Your Budget

Answer the following questions in your Money Nerve daily journal.

1. What are some of your beliefs that block financial success?

2. Write "Weekly Budget" at the top of one of your journal pages. Beneath that, write: "I am going to list all my money, in and out, for the week of _____ through _____. I will be completely honest and without judgment." Lay out *Income* and *Expenses* side by side.

3. After you lay out your budget, determine whether the final amount you have is an accurate representation of your cash on hand at the end of that week. How does it look?

4. Determine which expenses you can cut.

5. Begin to analyze the income side of your budgeting and find possible adjustments.

6. Write down the steps you will take to begin building an emergency fund.

7. Develop a contingency plan and write it down.

8. Continue writing in your daily journal.

5

Envision Your Financial Future

A Little Magic—Time to Dream

THROUGH BUDGETING, YOU ARE ABLE TO GET a sense of how your money flows. Now it is time for a little magic. The *magic* is the part of this process that starts to change your life. This chapter challenges you to define what you want in your life. It allows you to selfishly write down what you wish to have in your life. This is a special kind of selfishness; it is the kind that affects only you (and only in a positive way).

For many people, expressing what they want is a difficult thing. The media, advertisers, and our families tell us what we want (or what it means to be successful), but we rarely voice what it is that we truly want for ourselves.

I went to a comedy workshop on spontaneity that was supposed to be funny. It wasn't. In the first exercise, all the attendees were asked to pretend that they were kids again. They were then told to express what they wanted to be when they grew up. There was no laughter, no childlike dialogue. People were breaking down in tears.

One girl wanted to be a dancer, and all of the people in her life as a child told her that she couldn't be a dancer. She spent the exercise throwing a temper tantrum. She was kicking and screaming. The point of the exercise was to encourage limitless expression and playful thoughts, but many of the adults could only see their past from a negative point of view.

Children see the world without boundaries. Take the desire to be an astronaut, for example. Kids do not have to burden themselves with the knowledge of having to get a PhD, being physically fit, and having a specific mission in mind. Kids just dream.

As an adult, you will probably have to take action steps to move toward your dreams—and it's also important to first just dream. So for a moment, just dream. What would you like to be when you grow up? And now that you're an adult, you can savor the dream and think about the ways you can fulfill your dreams.

Let's say you dream about changing careers. Focus on your dream and know that there are steps you need to take to figure out how to accomplish that goal. One of my best friends wanted to become a real estate agent, so I bought him the materials he'd need to become licensed. Once the books arrived, he saw how much there was to study, and he changed his mind. He later told me that he felt like a failure. I disagreed. I told him it was important to celebrate the adjustments we make to our dreams. There are no wrong turns; there is only better information. Realizing the practicality of dreams and the effort it will take to fulfill them is how I define life.

Set Goals

Where Do You Want to Be?

"You are exactly where you want to be. If you weren't where you wanted to be, you would shift your priorities." I learned this idea at a conference I attended about eight years ago. The conference focused on evaluating our current position to determine how best to make changes and move forward. The statement was not well received. Most people in the audience were highly educated professionals, and they took offense to the idea that they had created their own mess on purpose. I was one of them. And then, through the course of the seminar, I realized I was exactly where I wanted to be.

At first, I thought, *That is not true at all.* I wanted more things and more money. My life wasn't bad, even though I had some debt from traveling to Africa, and I wanted to be free of debt. I finally came to realize that I was exactly where I was because I didn't understand what it was that I really wanted (or what I needed to do in order to make that dream a reality). I had never taken the time to lay it out.

I used to work in private accounting. I had a nice office, a secretary, and a good paycheck. But I wanted to become a CPA. I had taken all of the required courses, and I read that having my license would amount to a million dollars of additional income over my lifetime. So I quit my cushy job and worked three low-paying jobs at various CPA firms in order to get the necessary experience.

My goal was not to make more money. My goal was to get my license. Even though the goal of getting my license meant making more money in the long run, my CPA license was a specific enough goal. I could define the steps necessary to achieve it. I could have resented working at low-paying jobs, but I realized they were a means to an end I had set forth for myself.

Success Is a Journey

The dream of almost every improvisational comedian in the country is to land a spot as a cast member on Saturday Night Live. While writing this chapter, I bumped into an SNL cast member who had just heard she would not be picked up for another season. She had worked her whole life to achieve the goal of becoming an SNL cast member. Even though she was not asked back, she was grateful to have been on the show; she was not discouraged by her short time there. She realized that many people were disheartened because they never realized their dream, and she had achieved hers. She is a good example of the notion that success is a journey, not a destination.

More than a Snapshot

Sometimes a journey can comprise six, eight, or ten steps—and they are not always visible. We tend to make judgments based on a snapshot of a person's life. We may not take into consideration a person's history or potential for the future.

The Power of Now[8] was written by Eckhart Tolle, who is now a multi-millionaire. He was homeless and living on a park bench when he had an epiphany that turned into a best-selling book. If you had seen him living on a park bench, what would you have thought? The same people who thought he was a loser are now paying a thousand dollars to hear him speak.

A quote attributed to T.H. Thompson hangs above my computer: "Be kinder than necessary because everyone you meet is fighting some kind of battle." It reminds me to avoid the snapshot judgment.

Stop thinking that you are only as much as can be seen in a snapshot. You are not limited to the current snapshot of your life. There are too many things that can't be accounted for in a snapshot, including your

8   Tolle, Eckhart. *The Power of Now: A Guide to Spiritual Enlightenment.* Novato, CA: New World Library, 1999. Print.

ambition, dreams, luck, or love. You are so much more than your current situation. You are not just your bank account, your job, or your net worth. You are a combination of everything that is, was, and will be.

You are ready to change when you start to realize that you are not comfortable with your reality. One of my friends frequently asked me to lunch, and I agreed to go ... sometime. Finally, he said, "Hey, you are never going to go to lunch with me, so why don't you just admit it?" I argued with him at first, but then I realized he was right. Even though I wanted to grab a bite with him, I never made the time. I was choosing to work and refused to make the adjustment.

His pressure helped me realize I was a workaholic. I was choosing work over friendship. Until the day of that conversation, I was totally comfortable as a workaholic. Once I became aware of my tendency to choose work over friends, I slowed down and made some adjustments.

Protect Your Dreams

In some cases, not sharing your dreams can be a good thing. It is important to have a flame that burns so strong that other people can't blow it out. When people around me try to squash my dreams, I let them know I am not willing to listen to their negative outlook. I consciously look for ways to spend more time with a supportive network instead.

Create a group of like-minded people. It is a common idea that people who are successful surround themselves with successful people. It is not that you have to be surrounded by millionaires—spending time with people who have a positive attitude and are helpful and encouraging goes a long way.

There are ways to nurture yourself in an environment that is not supportive. We already talked about creating personal space for thirty minutes each day. If you have clearly defined goals, you will also have accomplishments to celebrate and milestones to focus on. So, in a way, nurturing yourself is cyclical. Creative space allows for dreams, which (when put into action) can change your reality in the way that you desire.

Successful people do not sit around thinking about how hard life is. They don't tell themselves that dreams are impossible. There is no reason you can't have all of the things you want. You have to have dreams. Dreams give people the passion to keep living. If you are passionate about what you do—whether it is writing, dancing, or being the best accountant you can be—you are going to be better connected to the people in your life. You will look forward to waking up each day and living your life.

Be Specific and Name It

Sing Your Song Out Loud!

I loved watching the episode of "Britain's Got Talent" in which Susan Boyle first took the stage. She told Simon Cowell she wanted to be a famous opera singer. The look on his face is the look that people try to avoid their entire life. It is the look that says, "That is impossible," or, "You have to be kidding me!" And then she started to sing. She amazed the audience, and she received a standing ovation. She became world renowned after that performance, and her CD went platinum. I want you to take this moment and sing your song! Tell the world what you want for your life!

"I [fill in your name] am remarkably passionate about _____
_____ and dream someday to _____!"

You did it! You laid the foundation for your future.

I work with a couple living on a fixed income. For years, they had a goal to buy a top-of-the-line Jacuzzi. They had a vision. They made a spot for it in their yard. They laid the foundation physically with cement, and they also laid the foundation on paper by making sure they had a budget for it. The foundation sat there for almost five years until they were able to purchase the best Jacuzzi money could buy.

That's the magic that I referred to in the first part of this chapter. I understand that it doesn't sound magical. Many people feel that magic is something that happens when you don't expect it. If you really knew the tricks employed by a magician to convince us something wonderful has happened, it wouldn't seem very magical either. Practical and simple financial steps create magic.

Ask for It

You should ask for the things you want every day. Asking for help puts you in a state of mind that helps you recognize you are not alone and there is something greater than you at work. Putting yourself in that mental state allows you to be humble enough to become aware of a larger reality. Whether you get to that state by praying daily or by being inspired by Napoleon Hill's *Think and Grow Rich*,[9] you unleash the power of your mind. The act of opening yourself up to the space you create every day through personal quiet time can help align you with your true self.

You never know how you may be affecting people with the choices you make. Money is no different. You may not be able to control when or how the rewards are paid back, but there is a karmic piggy bank somewhere in the universe with your name on it.

Karen is an accomplished wardrobe designer for movies. In some industries, such as the entertainment industry, companies have been known to take advantage of subcontractors who are willing to use their personal credit cards for company expenses (with the expectation of being promptly reimbursed). In this way, the company can ride out its debt and reimburse at its leisure. Ultimately, it would be financially preferable for such companies if people like Karen were not meticulous about tracking their expenses. When Karen was paid, she often forgot that some of the money was meant to pay off the credit card debt she had incurred.

---

9   Napoleon Hill, *Think and Grow Rich*. (Lexington: Soho Books, 2010).

Karen was putting herself at risk by fronting the money for the company. One small production ran out of money, leaving her stuck with their debt. When she came to my office the first time, she was frustrated because she was making good money but still had very high debt. She said she couldn't handle budgeting, and she was not good at keeping track of expenses. Karen finally realized that her flexibility with movie studios was hurting her own dreams, and she knew she needed to become clearer about what she really wanted.

We sat down to discuss her financial goals. She wanted to buy a house, have a savings account, and have no debt. Once her vision was clear, she was able to plan. She realized she should not take on personal liability for the studios by using her credit card. She had trouble budgeting because she had mixed the company's finances with her personal finances, and the lines were blurred. So she asked her present employer to give her a company credit card for expenses.

From that point on, all of the money she received was her own … and she was able to budget. The following year, she had over $100,000 in her savings account, and she was happy when she heard what she owed the IRS because she knew she had the money to pay her taxes. She would also have some left over for a down payment on a house. She said, "I can't believe how different my life is now." Once she focused on what she really wanted and asked for it, her financial life turned around.

Map Out New Financial Goals

It's Your Dream

Remember as you dream that it's *your* goal list, not your mother's list or your church's list or your child's list. If buying something for someone else or driving an expensive car is at the top of your list, try to determine why. Is it there because of guilt or insecurity? Or is it truly what you want to do? If you're not sure, ask yourself whether or not this choice is a result of your Money Nerve.

Think of what's really important to you. What do you want and why do you want it? Once you move away from the negative emotions that pinch your Money Nerve and head toward a more giving and empowering motivation, you may find that money will become a means to an end. I am not sure whether I have ever been passionate about accounting; however, I am passionate about helping other people. I help other people by being the best accountant I can be, which is also financially rewarding.

Pursuing your passion and following your dreams often results in financial rewards. When people are able to achieve financial stability, I love to celebrate their success. Are you ready to celebrate your success?

Call to Action

Celebrate Your Success!

Answer the following questions in your Money Nerve daily journal.

1. Take one minute and list ten things that you want to have in your life. Don't edit your thoughts. Do you have a pen? Go!

2. Look at the list you just created and write down where your financial emotions exhibit influence, where applicable.

3. Now that you know more about yourself and can identify your Money Nerve, it's time to create clear financial goals. Keep your dreams in mind as you record your new short-term, mid-range, and long-term financial goals:

   Short-term, immediate goals (today, this week, this month).

   Mid-term goals (this year, the next few years).

   Long-term goals (ten years, twenty years, retirement).

4. Choose one of the goals from each group (short-term, mid-term and long-term) and write out how budgeting will help you realize that goal.

5. Continue to write in your daily financial journal.

6

Prepare for Your Financial Journey

Your Financial Road Trip

IT'S ALMOST TIME TO GET ON THE road! There are a few more steps to take before you can begin your road trip to financial success, though. So far, you have decided to set a new course; you have explored emotions that can trigger your Money Nerve; you have addressed your fears; you have assessed your budget; and you have envisioned your future. Now you are ready to prepare for success!

In this chapter, you will set your intentions, assess your financial and emotional condition, and determine the specifics that will get you on your personal financial road. You are very close to getting what you want. This process is like planning a big trip. You figure out how to cover your costs; you collect the clothes and other items you will need for the trip; you plan your itinerary and determine how much cash you'll need to bring. When you have everything you need (including pre-journey jitters), get ready to hit the road!

Position Yourself

Decide to Get Ahead

I worked as an accountant in a clothing factory for a while. I was helping a company get off the ground, and I wanted to learn about the garment industry. Watching the factory workers clock in and out, I realized that few of them ever punched in at their scheduled start time or break time. There was a five-minute leeway in the time clock system, and almost everyone had figured out a way to beat the system. They could clock in five minutes late, start a break five minutes early, clock back in five minutes late, and punch out at the end of the day five minutes early. With a lunch and two breaks, they could gain forty minutes of free wages by playing the system.

Most of the people who worked in that factory seemed unhappy to be there, and beating the system appeared to give them some gratification. They acted as if they regretted every minute of work. They were living a paycheck-to-paycheck life that kept them from getting ahead.

You can stop the paycheck-to-paycheck mentality by looking at everyday spending. If you have ten dollars for lunch, do you spend the entire amount, or do you save a few bucks? The paycheck-to-paycheck mind-set could also be called the pocket-to-pocket mind-set. Keeping some money in your pocket when you could spend it all is a great way to start breaking the habit of feeling broke. Saving should become something that you do consistently in your everyday life. If you think you can save, you will. Breaking the cycle of empty pockets starts with a penny here and a penny there.

It is time for you to move up the ladder. You may be a great employee: you show up on time, and you complete tasks. Still, you may be wondering why other people are getting ahead of you at work (even though they have fewer skills and less time on the job). You may need to evaluate your attitude.

I have always hired people based on their attitude. I believe that surrounding myself with positive people makes me better. In that same clothing factory, the people I hired to work for me were some of the happiest people I have ever worked with—and every one of them went on to bigger and better careers. I knew that I was not going to stay in the same position for long, so I hired the best people possible. After all, I knew one of them would eventually have the opportunity to take over my job.

Envision Yourself Ahead

Most people are terrified to ask for a raise; they just wait to see whether their performance will be rewarded. If you envision what you want and tell yourself you deserve it—even if you request a raise and don't succeed—you are still grounded. You know what you are aiming for and can ask your boss what it would take to achieve your goals.

Before talking with your boss, be sure to evaluate your job performance. Perhaps you helped raise profits by 5 percent or cut spending by 10 percent. If you get along well with everyone, mention that. Raises are based on merit, and knowing your value helps you envision yourself getting ahead.

If you have never thought you could be a millionaire, will you become one? When I took my CPA exam, I knew I needed to pass with 76 percent. The first time I took the exam, I aimed for 76 percent and got 75 percent. I could not believe that I had failed. I knew that I had all of the knowledge necessary to complete the exam with a passing score; I had spent years preparing for it.

After I failed the exam, my friend said to me, "Why don't you aim for 100 percent instead of the 76 percent you know you need. See if you'll get a higher score." She pointed out that, when I had envisioned myself reaching 76 percent, I actually achieved 98 percent of what I was going for. As soon as my intention changed to getting every answer right, I passed the exam with ease.

Envision what you want and tell yourself it can happen. Sam had always wanted to own his own business. He didn't have specific details, he just knew he had a dream. Sam worked in a business park. There was no convenient place for a quick lunch. Each day, he'd come to work and think, "This place needs a sandwich shop." He realized there might be an opportunity to open his own business. He began to envision the details of his dream.

He started making plans and worked out all of the financial details for his own sandwich shop. He would offer a limited variety of panini sandwiches (two types of cheese, two types of meat), canned soda or bottled water, and two types of chips. He realized he should keep meal prices at ten dollars or less to attract lunch customers. He planned to lease four panini machines for six months at first (rather than purchase them) in case the restaurant didn't work out.

He needed a certain amount saved up before launching his plan. If the business took off in six months, he planned to continue. If not, he would get out without long-term debt. His exit strategy was in place. He saw a need and envisioned himself filling it. To his credit, Sam now owns a thriving sandwich shop.

Now that you have had some time to examine your Money Nerve and create new financial goals, what steps will you take to achieve them? We will never be emotionally or financially perfect. There is a world of difference between seeking to be okay and searching for joy in life. Allowing yourself to associate feelings of happiness and joy with your finances helps you train your mind. It will give your mind an emotional destination.

The idea of having real money come into your life may give you butterflies. Just because you may not know yourself as someone with a substantial amount of money does not mean that you cannot envision yourself with piles of cash. Current financial scenarios are static—they are what they are. Future financial scenarios are dynamic—they are changing one way with every dollar you spend and another way with every dollar you make. Envision what you want and make a commitment that you will have it (and that you deserve it).

Some people sabotage themselves because they are comfortable with their current story. Their mind is made up that nothing will change, and they are right. They would rather have their familiar message playing over and over than make any changes. You can smash your negative repetitive message by being specific in your choices. Nobody really knows how life will turn out. We can plan, set goals, and work toward those goals, but we might find that our life does not end up as planned.

If you examine quantum mechanics—the study of how the universe looks on the atomic and subatomic level—you will see that all matter is made up of energy. You are a giant bundle of potential energy, just waiting to be realized as something. When you define your something and believe in it, the universe will start to follow. Envision yourself ahead. Relish that vision; embrace it. Know that your current reality does not have to be your future reality. Aim for and have amazing financial freedom and financial success. You deserve it.

Assess Yourself

Create a Personal Inventory

It is also important to create an inventory of your abilities. Maybe you are in a job that only requires one or two of your many skills. Building a resume and keeping it current is a good idea—no matter how long you have been at your job and despite whether or not you plan to seek new employment. Acting as if you are preparing to look for another job can be an encouraging process in itself. It may motivate you to apply for an interesting new job or help you appreciate your present position. Just don't do it while you are at work!

The first part of a professional resume typically lists your background and skills. You probably have a resume from a past job interview. I have seen many resumes that read well, but they are not an accurate representation of the person applying for the job.

Beyond your professional resume, I encourage you to build a private resume. You won't use a private resume for a job interview; the purpose is to help you make an honest assessment of your skills and to focus on your intentions. The skills do not have to include which computer applications you are familiar with. They should, however, reflect the way you would describe your strengths to a friend (or the way a friend might describe you). "I can sell ice to an Eskimo," you might say, or, "I deal with difficult people easily."

List your five top skills:

1.

2.

3.

4.

5.

Through this process, you may find that you are already well suited for a position that you felt you could only obtain in the future. Conversely, you might realize that your area of expertise has been shifting over the years, and you are better equipped to branch out into a new field. Some people who complete this exercise find they fit perfectly in their current position and are ready to take it to the next level. Be careful to take into consideration market timing before you decide to barge into your boss's office requesting a raise, though.

The second part of your personal resume is a list of likes and dislikes. Don't hold back here. If you hate working for someone you cannot respect, write that down. It won't mean that every boss you have after this point will be an intellectual genius, but at least you know what you want. From this list, you should be able to analyze the career goals you have listed in previous chapters and determine whether they are in alignment with what works best for you.

Likes:

Dislikes:

Affirm Your Worth

If you were told that you were never going to amount to anything—or someone called you a loser when you were growing up—you may hear that naysayer's voice in your head. At some point, the voice in your head becomes your own voice. Even though someone else planted the seed, you nurture it by believing and repeating the negative message. Positive affirmations help change the message that plays over and over in your mind.

If you can envision your successful life, you can achieve it. Affirmations are mental muscle building. Just like workouts in a gym, progress takes time. You may not even notice there has been a change in your physical appearance until an outside person takes notice and gives you a compliment. In a similar fashion, affirmations will quietly take hold in your mind and begin to move your success vibrations to a higher level.

Remember the thirty minutes of personal space you've created? You can fill that space with your own positive thoughts. Many people think of affirmations (self-praise) as a form of egotism. While egotism is excessive focus on the self, affirmations simply build the ego in ways it is lacking. It takes practice. Learning to accept praise—self-praise or otherwise—is a skill. Most of us learned that it is not humble to accept praise. I used to discount others' compliments until I realized I was diminishing the gift they were giving me. Compliments are a gift, and learning to receive the gift is an important step in understanding affirmations. I tend to say the following affirmations daily:

"I am confident about my financial choices."

"I accumulate money and wealth."

Affirmations do not have to be comparative. You do not have to feel as though you are better or worse than anyone else during this process. Simply put, you thank yourself for being you, and you take stock of your accomplishments.

Determine Your Destination

Envision Your Next Steps

I have always known that I wanted to be a public speaker. About ten years ago, I started to think I would have an opportunity to have a positive effect on other people's finances. I did not know when that time would arrive; I only knew that I had to start preparing.

I was terrified of public speaking, so I confronted my fears. I started attending Toastmasters, and then I pursued stand-up comedy. Since then, I have done a lot of work on stage. Over time, I discovered information about myself that was contrary to what I had believed to be true about myself for years.

When I heard the phrase, "Life is a process of self-discovery," I wondered when my process would start. I now know that the precursor to self-discovery is envisioning and moving forward—even if that movement is difficult. My work on stage allowed for personal growth. Had I not envisioned being a strong public speaker, I would not have started the work.

Set your destination. Your destination does not have to be a giant leap. If you earned ten percent more than you do right now, what would you do with that additional money? Formulating a plan is the first step to long-term planning.

Remember your mental map from the beginning of this book. You wrote down short-term and long-term goals. Take a look at your notes. Armed with the new knowledge of why you make your financial choices, including the emotions that trigger your Money Nerve, reexamine your choices. Has anything changed? Don't hesitate to look to the future with thoughts that put you first. Assume for a minute that we live in a limitless world without judgment. Would your vision of success remain the same?

The larger the gap between your vision and your reality, the more simple and cautious your first steps must be.

Attitude

Attitude is an important factor for progress. Counting inventory used to be a requirement to get your CPA certificate, so people often called my office to offer to work for free if I would confirm in writing that they had counted inventory.

When two of these young people who wanted to become CPAs approached me a few years ago, I had just landed a job to count inventory. I invited them to start the next day. The main thing I was able to count that day was the number of times they complained. They said, "This is boring. When do we get to stop?" Their attitude needed adjustment. If you have a specific goal, and there are requirements involved to get there, you need to be willing to embrace those requirements with an understanding that they are an integral part of your journey.

If you have pressing financial obligations, you might not be able to take a large leap. You may have to bide your time to make sure that you have a game plan in place. Maybe that plan includes taking a few extra courses at a local college or seeking out new employment while you still have the job that you hate. Your job then becomes a means to an end.

People often tell me I was lucky I chose to be a CPA. It was not luck. I had a vision based on my passions and skills and worked hard to turn it into a reality. I have had my own practice for many years, and it has evolved over time. I shifted away from partners who did not share my financial perspective. I have a solid staff of people because I reward their value. Our clients love us because we have great attitudes and are client-focused. Maybe I am lucky, and maybe we can all create the foundation for our own luck with hard work and focus.

Create Detailed Financial Maps

Many people say that you only need to believe in something to make it come true. Here is something that should come as no secret to most of you: success requires hard work. Yes, I believe that it is important to visualize your future in order to make changes. However, if your reality keeps reflecting something different than what you envision, you may need to put in a few more hours. If you keep thinking you should be better off financially without doing all you can to make that happen, there will be no change.

The more you practice financial mapping and budgeting, the easier it will be to practice mental mapping. There is a direct relationship between the two types of mapping. (Please note, however, that mental mapping does not guarantee financial success.)

Every comic I know wants to be a huge success. It takes more than being funny to get there. For instance, comics need head shots and videos of their sets to promote themselves to potential venues. In order to get the right video, they need a video camera for taping and a computer for editing (provided they are capable of editing). They can pay someone to do the editing, but the editors may cut the jokes wrong and ruin the punch lines. They usually have a specific mental map, but often, they do not make the connection between mental mapping and financial mapping. They have not taken the time to understand the financial consequences of their mental mapping.

If your mental mapping (destination) indicates that you want to go to the family reunion, you also need to look at your financial map (ways and means). Should you take a car? How much will it cost for gas versus flying? If you drive, how many nights will you need to pay for a hotel? If you don't make the plans to get there, you may find yourself experiencing the event vicariously through the people who did map out their plans.

Once you map out your financial needs, you can begin to adjust your mental map. It is important to be both specific and realistic when you envision your financial future. Too often, people say that they want to be the best at something, or they say that they want to be rich. Mental mapping is about specifics. How can you measure best? The more specific you are, the more tangible and measurable your outcomes will be.

Financial mapping needs to be practical. Being realistic is important, especially in difficult financial times. Now, more than ever, you need to be honest with yourself financially. It is easier to be unaware in prosperous times. Unfortunately, you are no longer in a financial scenario in which you can remain unconscious about your finances.

Once you are specific with your process of envisioning, you have to get to work. The work will help you define how realistic your visions can become. You shouldn't edit your dreams and passions. They are your dreams, and sometimes they just remain dreams. You start to understand the difference when you test the waters.

When I was talking with a friend recently, he said that, when he was younger, his dream was to become a singer. Everyone else told him he should find another dream. He truly was not a good singer. He was not happy with the feedback, and he realized that he really didn't have the voice to turn his interest into a career. Still, he could sing passionately in the shower.

At a certain point, practicality tells you to find a different outlet to base your earnings on. Sometimes, a person's mental mapping changes because constant frustrations or disappointments keep popping up. There is nothing wrong with changing direction.

Even the most amazing singers hit a few sour notes when starting out. It takes years of practice before you can hit every note. Taking steps toward your dreams moves them away from the realm of the intangible and toward reality. Even if you don't understand all of the steps it will take to achieve your goals, working toward them helps you determine which goals are realistic.

Your mapping is specific to your personality. Once I know my mental map, I may look at my financial map and realize that I have to make adjustments. If you look at your list of short-term and long-term goals, you can determine whether the issue relates to mental mapping or financial mapping. If your list includes paying off your debt, taking a vacation, and saving money for a down payment on a house, you will be better served by focusing on financial mapping. If you want to become a doctor or start a foundation to combat hunger, your focus will fall into the mental mapping arena.

Time It Right

Timelines Are Personal

There are many factors involved that differentiate one person's timeline from another's. Comparing yourself to others is not an effective guidepost. You may feel you should be at a higher financial level (or working with a certain company), and the change just hasn't happened. Then, all of a sudden, for no rhyme or reason, the change occurs. You are presented with the opportunity you had been searching for. Timing is everything.

One of my clients is a psychotherapist for a county and manages several facilities. She has worked to create her own practice, which she happens to find much more rewarding. She is slowly building a private practice while working at her primary job. We created a three-year budget for her so that she knows how much she will need in order to be able to walk away from her other job. Through long-term budgeting, she can track her financial journey.

She created the vision to build her own practice. She put in the work to understand what it took to run a business, and she spent time building up her clientele. Just as she was about to take the leap, the local economy tanked. She decided to extend her salaried income until the economy leveled out, giving her own practice a better chance of success.

Knowledge of exactly where you are in relationship to your goals helps you make specific choices. It allows you to become more aware of how to budget your time and money so that you can balance paying the bills and laying the foundation for the future.

You might dislike the current location of your financial journey—not knowing that the next turn may bring you exactly what you need. You may be going through a part of your life that you'd rather avoid, yet you could be a small detour away from getting to where you truly want to be.

It can be difficult to fully grasp where you are on your personal financial timeline. Sometimes, the fastest route is not a straight line. Don't beat yourself up if your journey doesn't take you where it took someone else you know. Don't get discouraged. Sometimes, life has unexpected things in store for you. You might be planning to get a degree when your child gets severely ill and needs your time and care instead. Taking care of your child is exactly the right place to be—even if it delays your plans.

Being sidetracked doesn't mean you are on the wrong track. Maybe you feel you are zigzagging. Be aware that there may be an invaluable lesson to learn for the future. At least you're still moving and doing exactly what you have to do in order to get where you want to be.

You might also want to consider where your ego stands on the journey through life. When we are young, many of us think about becoming rich and famous. As we age and gain perspective on what is most important to us, we begin to let go of some of the desires we had in our youth. A decrease in ego-driven needs does not have to correlate to a decrease in the drive to achieve. Many people adjust to a service-to-others mentality rather than service-to-self frame of mind.

Consider Market Factors

Timing can be personal in many areas of our individual financial goals … and then there are market factors that are beyond our control. Let's say that your mental mapping sees you as the highest grossing real estate agent in the country, but you live in a rural area. You might be the hardest working real estate agent, you might make the most money on a relative scale, but you will not be the highest grossing real estate agent. The property values in smaller markets are not going to support your idea. Information leads to adjustments, even in mental mapping. Once you understand that there are parameters set in place that you cannot adjust, you might make the adjustment to say that you will be the highest grossing real estate agent in your area.

Market cycles should also be considered when it comes to your choices. One friend's wife is certain they are going to be making more money soon, and she wants to move into a bigger house. The signs are definitely there; I think they will be making more money as well. A few years back, they could have easily qualified for a loan. Now, because of tighter rules, my mortgage broker tells me only one in about forty people requesting a loan is able to qualify. This new cycle means they will probably have to wait to buy a bigger house.

You Are on Your Way

You have started the process. You are doing the work. You are readying yourself for your financial journey. You have some psychological understanding of your roadblocks. You have worked through the emotional blocks to your financial success. You know you want something different, and you have made the commitment to change.

Take a look at the information that you have used to challenge your previous mind-set. Whether you recognize it or not, you have shifted. You are at the point where you cannot un-know what you know. This is the exciting part: you are on your way to financial success, and you have created this possibility for yourself. No one but *you* could have created this. Let the journey truly begin.

Call to Action

Map Out Your Success

Answer the following questions in your Money Nerve daily journal.

1. Review your personal resume and write down adjustments you can make to turn it into a job resume.

2. Begin to affirm your success daily. Write down the affirmation you will use.

3. Without judgment, write out your limitless personal financial vision.

4. Use your personal resume and your personal financial vision to create a detailed map—both mental and financial. Remember: your mental map is where you want to go, and your financial map helps you figure out how to fund your journey. Make sure you are specific with deadlines and dollar amounts.

5. Remember to keep up with your daily journal.

7

Nervous?

Step by Step

Make Emotional Adjustments

Is your Money Nerve setting your limits? Do you tell yourself that if things change, you might end up with a life that you don't deserve? Or are you so exhausted by recurring patterns that you can't see yourself in any other circumstance?

Equipped with the knowledge gained from the previous chapters, you've begun—or *can* begin—to make the emotional adjustments necessary to take control of your Money Nerve. You can move more easily toward the financial future you envision.

There is no way to fully conquer your Money Nerve. You may work through a pattern of fear at your place of employment only to have fear show up in another area. Having worked through the pattern and dealt with the emotion, you will be better equipped to handle new scenarios.

Be careful that you do not overwhelm yourself. This knowledge should not become debilitating. If you start to feel overwhelmed, you need to stop, take a breath, and remind yourself that self-discovery is a lifelong process.

Some of your attitudes toward money may have been helpful in the past ... and they still may be necessary for your emotional stability. You will make some discoveries that might help you realize that you are living with a mental map that no longer serves you.

Choose Happiness

Many studies have analyzed the connection between wealth and happiness. After reviewing several major studies, Melanie Greenberg, in a recent article in The Mindful Self-Express, comes to the conclusion that money is only one ingredient in our happiness quotient. She notes:

> Money does not make as much difference as we think. When researchers asked people earning $25,000 how much happier they would be if they earned $55,000, most people said their happiness would more than double. However, when actual happiness scores were compared, those earning $55,000 were only about 10 percent happier. So, money does make you happier, but mostly only a little.[10]

---

10   Melanie Greenberg, PhD, "Is Money the Secret to Happiness?" *Psychologytoday. com.* The Mindful Self-Express, (Sept. 2012): accessed October 3, 2012, http://www.psychologytoday.com/blog/the-mindful-self-express/201209/is-money-the-secret-happiness.

To move us away from the materialistic aspects of wealth, perhaps we should focus our attention on what we do with that wealth—however much it is. By gaining perspective and finding joy in, say, helping others financially (or spending quality time with family on a vacation), we learn to savor the ways we engage our money in the world.

My friend is continually in a good mood. She runs her own business, lives with a high-stress husband and three rambunctious young boys, and always seems upbeat and happy. When I call her for advice, she listens for a few minutes and usually gives a reply that sounds more like the Dalai Lama than a businesswoman from the Midwest. When it comes to emotions, her favorite saying is, "Nothing can make us feel any different than how we choose to feel."

Choose happiness. Like my friend, I believe that we can learn to better relish life's moments and savor our experiences more. Dr. Heidi Grant Halvorson, in her recent article in Living, reached the same conclusion. And she goes a step further by putting this concept into action by making a plan. She says:

> People are, on average, 200–300% more likely to succeed if they use [advance] planning. So, if you want to remember to savor, you could make plans like the following:
>
> If I am eating, **then** I will remember to do it slowly and think about how my food tastes.
>
> If I have a success at work, **then** I will tell my friends and family about what happened.
>
> If I see something beautiful, **then** I will stop and soak it in, and feel fortunate to have seen it.
>
> Make savoring life's little pleasures your goal. Create plans for how to inject more savoring into each day, and you will significantly increase your happiness and well-

being—and, in many cases, your own wealth. And if your riches aren't growing, then savoring is still a great way to truly appreciate what you *do* have.[11]

Being able to choose your emotions is not something that happens overnight. Emotions are one of life's strongest motivating forces, so it takes time to learn to harness them. Through years of hard work and adjustments, I have learned to take control of my emotions and my Money Nerve.

You, too, can shift from a reactive state to a proactive state. Through repetition and patience, you will begin to lay the emotional foundation for your financial success and feel your success before it happens. The first steps involve envisioning your future, assessing your abilities, and moving into a detailed financial plan of action.

Change Your Internal Story

Money is not the only measure for change. There are immeasurable changes that may make you a millionaire in the future. If you know you are on a path—and you are aware of your progress toward your goals—it doesn't matter whether your changes have yet to be monetized. You are building a life resume. There are things you do that you can record on paper (monetarily or otherwise), and there are things you do that make you who you are.

If you are a homeless man sitting on a bench writing a book called *The Power of Now,* your reality does not reflect your potential. Living with intention helps you focus on your goals and ignore the judgment of others. You can only live one life: your own. You cannot live the life you should have lived or the life others think you should live. Learning to enjoy your own life is an important step toward a more focused life.

---

11   Heidi G. Halvorson, "Why More Money Probably Won't Make You Happy." *Positivelypositive.com.* Living, (9 Mar. 2012): accessed October 3, 2012, http://www.positivelypositive.com/2012/03/09/money-happy/.

Change your emotional make-up so that you are comfortable having money in the bank. A lot of people quickly drain their bank account of any additional money so that they can get back to living the story they know how to tell: the I'm-always-broke story. Change your story by telling yourself, "I feel really comfortable with money."

Make Healthy Financial Decisions

Shift

Harry was sitting on the fence. He had promised his employees that if they all took a pay cut, he would not fire anyone. After he made the promise, the economy changed dramatically—even beyond what he had already anticipated. He realized that he was going to lose his entire business if he didn't let go of a few employees. Harry could not bring himself to make the choice between breaking his word and losing his business.

He asked me to help him solve his dilemma. I asked the basic questions first. Do you want your company to go out of business? Are you willing to lose your credit and personal investment in your business? Are you willing to change your mind about breaking your word?

I did an analysis for him and showed him that his indecision was equivalent to actively choosing to lose his business. Presented with all of the facts—even though his inevitable decision made him physically ill—Harry realized that, by continuing to sit on the fence, everyone would lose.

In this case, Harry ended up letting go of most of his employees. By getting off the fence, he was able to stay in the game. He at least had a small business that continued to be viable (rather than a large business that would have failed). It would have been much more difficult for him to seek new clients if he had to restart his business. After less than a year, he started to win new contracts, and his services were again in high demand—so much so that he began rehiring the employees he had let go six months earlier.

Regardless of the scenario, the process of making healthy financial decisions is the same. Knowing the financial point of view of my clients helps me tailor the conversation to accommodate the way they handle information. When I see a place where they are stuck and see they haven't been able to move past it, I ask them whether they want to make a shift.

For instance, if a client continually overspends, I ask whether he has set up a budget. Sometimes, I get answers such as, "I don't believe in budgeting. The money will eventually come." If he feels comfortable where he is and is not prepared to make a change, I don't walk him through the entire process of making healthy financial decisions.

Harry was ready to shift. Not all of my clients are. Some of them in similar positions are not able to come to a decision. They are not emotionally and mentally able to make a decision and take action. They may need to take time to carefully consider their options. Or they are simply unable to face the facts. We discuss the amount of time they need to review or come to terms with the facts, and we have a follow-up conversation later to see whether they are ready to make a shift. What is surprising is that many people will directly admit, "I am not willing to change."

Learn to Pause

I want to accomplish one thing when I am working with clients who face a difficult financial decision: I want them to have a mental "hiccup" rather than to respond automatically. A mental pause is necessary to help them realize that the record that has been playing in their mind is no longer accurate or necessary.

A new client always complained he was broke. The truth was that he was not budgeting and had no idea what his financial position was. He told me that he found comfort saying he was broke—even though we both knew that he was exhausted, frustrated, and not broke. His mental mapping had trained him to say it over and over. He was only comfortable with the repetition. Once he recognized this, he stopped saying he was broke.

It takes time to get to a point where you are able to embrace this process of openness and evaluation. Once you do, you can take the steps to replace your story with your truth.

Track Emotional Responses

Notice Your Money Nerve

You can physically feel your Money Nerve. If you have been keeping notes in your journal, you are more aware of your body and the physical cues that can occur when you deal with your finances. Reflecting on your physical being and your emotional response will help you become more aware of how your Money Nerve affects you in the moment.

Becoming more aware, however, does not mean you will become an emotional zombie when it comes to finances. I will probably always get an upset stomach if I get an overdraft notice. I hate to be overdrawn. Decisions that take into consideration the Money Nerve beforehand help mitigate their effects on your day-to-day life. Knowing your emotions helps you take appropriate actions so that you can deal with your finances in the best way possible.

I realize this process of self-discovery isn't easy. If it were, everyone would be debt free and have enough money in the bank to live comfortably. Facing your Money Nerve can be difficult and frightening. Let's say, at this point, you are not yet taking steps to make your life better out of fear. Are you willing to experience the fear and still push through it? Most people go toward change kicking and screaming. They may think there is less risk when they box themselves up and resist change. The environment around us is changing so quickly that adaptation is a necessity. Those who are willing to make changes by being honest and facing their emotions are the people who are moving toward success.

Taking an emotional inventory in the moment is the first step. This self-reflection helps you become aware of how you feel when you make financial decisions. If you are having difficulty figuring out how your Money Nerve affects your finances, think back to moments during a single day when you had to make a financial decision. Choosing to buy coffee for a friend or waiting to make a credit card payment may have triggered your Money Nerve. Ideally, you'll start to note it at the end of every day as part of your mental mapping and reflection.

Recognize Fear of Success

Does the thought of success make you feel uneasy? With success just around the corner, many people feel their Money Nerve being pinched and run in the other direction. They may truly want to have money, but they begin to experience feelings of insecurity and fear.

I liken the feeling to a sort of financial stage fright. I have experienced stage fright more often than I care to recall. Each time, I pushed through the fear and took the stage. I now know the process of facing my fear is not going to harm me. Similarly, remind yourself that financial success has been your goal (and you are capable of handling it).

Prosperity Brings Responsibility

Pressure to Perform

In many instances, increased earnings mean increased pressure to perform. One of my clients recently received a promotion that came with a nice bonus and added responsibilities. The new responsibilities included preparing and delivering a weekly meeting in front of department heads. She felt such discomfort with public speaking that she left the job after a few months for a position at another company that paid less.

Visibility and exposure often accompany an increase in earnings. Whether you own your own company or are part of an organization, more money can mean a bigger spotlight is directed at you. The spotlight may expose weakness, or it may serve to highlight your strengths.

Hopefully, you did an accurate personal inventory in the previous chapter. By putting your personal resume down on paper, you expose yourself to your own truth. That way, when you do have a spotlight on you, you will already know where your strengths and weaknesses lie. You will know whether you are up to the task or not; fear and anxiety will be limited. You may need more time to acquire the skills you need to be competitive in the new field.

Let's say you are a teacher. You want more money. You like teaching, so you decide to obtain a master's degree. You will have to invest in your education, which may mean taking on more debt. You will spend additional time studying, attending classes, and writing a thesis. Once you earn that degree, you will most likely be given more responsibilities.

If you want more money still, you could pursue a doctorate. You will have to spend even more money, study even harder, and publish a dissertation. Most people don't see the correlation between earning more money and the amount of responsibility associated with the increased earnings. If they did, they might realize that they are not willing to make all the necessary changes.

Use Your Dreams to Energize You

A lot of entrepreneurs are passionate about their ideas. They have tremendous energy and the ability to translate their enthusiasm to others. And then, after about six months, they realize they need to learn to run a business. When they find out what it takes to build and maintain their ideas, they often become bored or overwhelmed.

The amount of time and energy it takes to actually realize your dreams can be draining. A friend of mine has been trying to start a medical device company for the last year. He is working with a doctor who has developed products to help monitor babies during pregnancy. When my client talked about how excited he was to bring the products to market, the room seemed to become brighter. After about a year, he set up an appointment to see me. His energy was completely drained. Once he began to analyze the marketplace, he realized the huge barriers to entry. As we started to discuss his ideas to help pregnant women, his spark returned. He had not returned to his source of inspiration for a long time because he was so caught up in the process and challenges of making his dream a reality.

He was a good businessperson and an excellent salesman, and he knew that the business would be a success. He did not have to find funding or present his ideas for approval. What he did need to do was write down the steps necessary to achieve his business goal—essentially, he had to create a business plan. Seeing what he wanted to achieve and quantifying the steps necessary to get there propelled him forward. He is currently making inroads with hospitals across the country, and he is smiling from ear to ear.

Change Helps Fulfill Dreams

My experience shows that people are much more content in their current position after evaluating the responsibilities that come with higher earnings. They may complain about the amount of money they are earning, but frequently, they are unwilling to pursue further education or take on new job requirements to earn a higher salary.

Realize that you are not a victim of your circumstances. Your decisions have led you to this point. You have accomplished what you have chosen to do. You are executing your decisions perfectly. Maybe you need to adjust your choices. Nervous or uneasy feelings often surface around the idea of getting more money. The fear does not manifest itself because you are afraid of the actual, physical money. The fear is about the changes you need to make to *acquire* more money.

If you strive to achieve more—and you take on additional responsibilities—change will find you. When I went into accounting,

I did so in order to avoid interacting with anyone. The better I became, the more I had to talk to people. Now I sit down and talk to people and give speeches in front of large crowds. I never would have dreamed it possible. Once you start making changes, anything is possible.

It is important to be aware that there will be multiple changes along the way to fulfill your vision. Most people assume the worst is going to happen and feel they need to have all of the answers before they start out on a new path. Nobody has all of the answers.

I often tell people that I am not the smartest accountant in the world, but I ask the right questions and know when I don't know the answer. In other words, I am not always going to have the answer at the tip of my finger. For many people, the fear of not being in control is debilitating. If you fear that the spotlight will be too strong for you, you can ask for help.

Schedule Time to Contemplate

If you have difficulty finding time to sit and contemplate, try the following strategy. I had trouble making time for myself, and I used to get upset when clients would run fifteen minutes late or cancel their appointments. Now I relish their lateness or cancellations. I see this as extra me time. I can return phone calls, check my e-mails, meditate, or do absolutely nothing.

I've taken an annoyance and turned it into a win-win situation. If the client arrives on time, I win; if not, I still win. If you have an extremely busy schedule, you can use the downtime created by waiting rooms or late appointments to reflect on your Money Nerve. You do not have to have your eyes closed and your palms facing up in order to do some simple reflection.

Once I recognized my Money Nerve, I started making changes. In the first few years of my accounting practice, I had a strong physical reaction if a client ever said he or she was thinking about leaving me. The insecurity I felt (assuming I had not done a good job) caused my stomach to turn. I took steps to fight off that feeling by spending extra hours trying to make everything right. It cost me quite a bit of time and money. Eventually, I realized that my reaction was based on avoiding failure. It was an emotion I had been carrying with me since childhood, and it did not accurately reflect my current perspective. Now, a simple conversation either turns around or closes a client relationship for me.

When I look at all of the fear-based decisions I made when I was younger, I am amazed at some of my choices. It is easy to look back at past financial decisions and judge yourself harshly, yet you made them with all of the financial information you had available at the time. Once you begin recognizing the emotions attached to your financial decisions, you can begin making better choices in the moment. The knowledge of the presence of these emotions may affect more than just your finances.

Do the Work

Now comes the difficult part. Many people make it quite far before deciding to quit. Are you going to continue to complain about your finances, or are you going to do something about them? You can read this book and find it informative, but if you have not done your budgeting, created a personal resume, or completed the Call to Action sections of this book, you are not doing the necessary work to address your Money Nerve.

Most of you reading this book are entertaining the idea of changing your financial lives. You have to commit to the work in order for change to happen. Here's the great news: if you do the work, you'll change your financial future. When you are so frustrated with your situation that you are willing to do the work to seek change, you will.

I was recently at a self-help seminar, and I realized that many of the attendees were not really seeking change. They were looking for a third party to tell them they were okay. They wanted validation that their scenario was good enough.

You are the only person responsible for your financial scenario. If you are blaming others, it's time to recognize you are making the choice to blame rather than change. In order to change, it often has to be more painful to stay in the same situation than to try something new. You may have to get to a boiling point in order to alter your way of thinking.

You can do it.

Call to Action

Assess Your Financial Relationships

Answer the following questions in your Money Nerve daily journal.

1. Consider a situation you face in which a key financial decision must be made and complete the following exercise:

    List the pros and cons of the situation.

    Write out the most likely outcomes to each possible decision you could make.

2. Take an inventory of the emotions that pinch your Money Nerve when you do the following things:

    Pay bills.

    Check account balances.

    Misplace your wallet or purse.

3. Based on your knowledge of the emotions behind your Money Nerve, complete the following exercises:

    Revise your short-term goals.

    Revise your mid-term goals.

    Revise your long-term goals.

4. Write in your daily journal.

8

Find the "Financial You"

You Are Not Alone

IT'S TIME TO BECOME CONSCIOUS OF WHO you really are—time to really be aware. It's time for you to actively participate in your financial future. Know that you are not alone.

In this chapter, we will focus on identifying your priorities. We will look at ways to gain support from others that will help hold you accountable for your own goals. We will explore financial issues with people in your inner circle, including your immediate family.

You are ready to manifest change in your life. Go forth and bring about that which you desire: a healthy financial future. The time is now.

Deal with Your Finances

You are not the only one struggling with your financial issues. You may find more opportunities for discussion or working on your finances with others when an acquaintance shares a personal financial scenario.

It is not that you enjoy knowing other people are suffering just like you; it is that you are taking comfort in knowing that there are allies out there who will help you through your difficulties. If you are overwhelmed in a certain area, you can look for help.

Be aware that the simplest financial concept often seems incredibly difficult to understand. Take the concept of interest rates. If you know what they are—and many of you do because you are forced to pay them—the concept is easy to understand. It seems almost commonplace. But if you do not know what interest rates are, you can become immobilized.

If you are dealing with interest rates, tax withheld from paychecks, balanced budgets, or debits and credits, for instance, your financial brain may become overwhelmed. Don't feel alone. Many people struggle with financial concepts.

Not dealing with your finances makes it much harder to move forward. If you let money define you as a person, you are doing yourself a disservice. Finances are part of your life, but they are not you. As you gain more control of your finances, you become less defined by them. When the finances become understandable and manageable, you can move forward more easily.

Identify Your Priorities

Priorities are not limited to material things. A priority could be that you want to spend more time with your kids. It does not always have to be something that involves money—it's about finding the right value for you.

When I first started working and money was tight, I had a maid. It was more important to me to have fresh sheets every week and come home to a clean house than to buy expensive groceries. I ate a lot of rice and soup, but my pressed sheets made me feel like a king.

I once knew someone who worked for UPS. He seemed like a smart guy, and I wondered whether his job was fulfilling enough for him. One day, he announced he was retiring! I was shocked. He looked about thirty-five years old.

He told me he started working there when he was eighteen, worked for twenty years, and earned a good pension from UPS. He had a couple of kids and wanted to spend his afternoons with his kids. So every morning (for twenty years), he left for work around four o'clock in the morning and returned home around three o'clock in the afternoon. He had a clear picture of his priorities.

Create a Financial Support Group

Partner Up

Sharing your new financial journey with others can help keep you on track. You can start with a partner or build a team. Keeping a budget actually becomes fun with a partner because you can compete with one another to see who keeps track of receipts best or spends the least.

You might call each other up and say, "Hey, let's go through our receipts." Or you might say, "Let's make a list of free things to do on a Saturday night." You could take your partner to lunch to celebrate a zero balance on her credit card—use a discount coupon and pay cash!

Ultimately, when I work with a partner on certain things, it's easier to achieve my goals. I get support and encouragement. Also, it's a great way to be held accountable. Find a partner who shares a similar financial vision or wants to join you in the budgeting journey.

Actively Seek Support

Turn back to your personal resume. When you find an area of finances you do not handle well (which causes you to ignore that area), start looking for support. You do not need to hang out at coffee shops looking for someone who loves to budget. Support comes in many different forms. Support can be an application on your phone or computer that prompts you to detail your expenses, or it could be an online discussion board where you can post questions about finances.

You can either walk through this process by yourself, or you can find someone to play devil's advocate and ask you the tough questions that need to be addressed. It is more difficult to think of alternatives to your current mental map when you attempt this process on your own. Your financial partners—people in your life who have a direct effect on your finances—are necessary partners on your road to financial change.

It is also important to work with groups or individuals who play no direct role in your finances. I became aware of the emotions that triggered my Money Nerve through feedback. I called a few people I knew who always seemed to be striving to achieve more, and I asked them to be a part of my financial success group. We were a group of people with different skills, working toward separate goals—and we all wanted our financial lives to improve.

I was willing to ask my support group whether the emotions behind my Money Nerve were warranted. I didn't trust my gut. I was mentoring people in accounting and advising my clients on important financial matters even as I struggled with some of the same issues. I could not ignore my personal finances because they were affecting me physically. I knew the advice I was giving others was sound, but I wasn't utilizing it for my own finances.

I worked for a company that was not paying me what I was owed. I told a member of my financial success group that I knew I was being underpaid. I was part of a profit-sharing arrangement, yet I never saw an end-of-year reconciliation and was certain I had contributed more to the profit than I was being paid for. He suggested I keep track of all the work I did in writing.

At first, I refused to do what I perceived as extra work (plus, I felt it was someone else's job!). And then I realized it was a simple solution. At the end of the year, I walked into my boss's office and showed him I was due an extra 35,000 dollars. With the paperwork in hand, he could only do one thing: write me the check.

Instead of complaining that I was a victim who wasn't receiving his due, I took a simple action. I needed an outside source to show me the way. Since then, I have been determined to be the source for others' financial enlightenment.

Your ultimate goal is to have peace of mind. As you start to deal with sticky financial situations in the moment, you pave a smooth road for the future. To make forward progress, you need to get the basics down first. Understanding how your Money Nerve gets pinched will help you look at your finances in a new way.

Choosing appropriate people to offer you feedback is important. For the most part, we would love our family to provide us with honest and supportive feedback. However, they are rarely the best choices. People who love you and want to protect you are generally too emotionally attached to give an objective perspective. They may see themselves in you and answer questions that are specific to your life, but from their own point of view, which may not wholly fit your situation. The irony is that the same people we want in our support groups are often the wrong people for the job.

Address Finances with Business and Personal Partners

Take the Initiative

Financial partners are the people in your life who have the greatest effect on your personal finances. These people could be business partners, spouses, significant others, or family members you're in a business relationship with.

What most of us neglect to do is engage our financial partners so that we are on the same page. Whether we are talking about our personal problems or our interpersonal problems, the most frequent choice is to avoid confrontation. Eventually, avoiding financial issues will come back to bite you. Financial problems tend to recur along the same lines over and over.

As you become more aware of your emotions and what triggers your Money Nerve, you will be able to be more understanding of your partner's Money Nerve. You want to have a conversation based on your improved understanding of the person you are dealing with. You may still be annoyed and even upset by the reactions of others—and you now have some tools to deal with your situation.

I've met with several engaged couples who realized the importance of discussing finances before getting married. One young man wasn't sure how to address the issue with his fiancée without hurting her feelings. He ended up saying, "I've arranged a meeting with my accountant so we can discuss how things change when we are married." She hadn't thought of that and felt it was a good idea.

Other couples never communicate about their finances. Connie told James she had sent checks for the previous year's estimated tax payments. He found out she hadn't when a lien was filed against him. It was a shock to him to discover Connie was unable to deal with taxes. Instead of responding with anger, he decided to handle their taxes in the future.

Don't get upset when you are the one taking the initiative to address finances. Someone will always care more about being financially secure. I consider my finances my most important household chore to manage. For example, I am a little self-righteous about handling the finances, and I do not want to give up that part of the decision-making process.

Become Aware of Assumptions

All financial partnerships should be founded on clear expectations. Addressing assumptions about who should be doing what is often the first step. Yet we tend not to talk about financial expectations with our life partners.

You may be reluctant to address finances with your partner because of the emotions that you know will surface during the process. If you address difficult feelings about money either of you might have (such as depression or guilt), you will be less likely to avoid this necessary conversation.

You may find that qualities you appreciate about yourself can negatively affect your partner. Understanding each other's emotions can help you make sense of your choices and help you both make wise ones.

If you make the time to deal with difficult situations, you won't have to deal with them during a crisis. Two guys were going to buy a pharmacy and asked me to evaluate the business. I spoke with each partner separately, and Kevin said his biggest concern was his partner's wife. He felt she was a know-it-all, and he was concerned she would try to tell him how to run the business.

We sat down with the other partner, and I said, "Kevin will be your partner, not your wife. She can't tell him how to run the business." He said, "Oh, she is a little pushy. I will talk with her and handle that." They fixed the situation before it became a problem.

Talking Points for Partners

Is one saving while the other spends? How honest are you with each other? Finances can be hard to talk about. If you have no problem discussing finances with your financial partner, I would say you are in the minority.

You might find that your financial partner disagrees with areas outside of finances that you would rather avoid than address. I am not saying you should use budgeting as an excuse to figure out whether you want to have kids or not, but such talks may lead to more serious conversations. You can always set parameters at the beginning of the conversation by saying that you would like to keep the discussion to matters of finance.

After analyzing your relationship with your financial partner, you may find that it is exactly what you need. If you hate to deal with budgeting, you might be happy that your partner is a controller. I think it is important to affirm each other's positive attributes. Tell your partner that you appreciate when he or she takes care of bills or makes adjustments to your cell phone plan (just as you would thank them for handling any non-financial matters).

Involve Your Kids

I recently climbed several peaks in Colorado. As I got close to the summit of each peak, those who had reached the top before me were hiking back down the mountain. The hikers stopped for a few minutes to give suggestions about the path and to explain the conditions near the peak. Having someone who has previously been on the path impart his or her knowledge is invaluable.

Parents often forget to include their children in financial discussions. Talk with your children about financial responsibilities and explain the financial workings of your home. Involving your children in financial discussions is an important step to help ensure they become financially aware.

All too often, parents want to protect their children from financial realities. There is a cost to giving your children whatever they want, and it is more than the collective price tags of the items purchased. Without demonstrating financial consequences, there is little incentive for your children to mature financially.

The families I have worked with that have the most financially competent children do not just give money to their children. They set guidelines for allowances and discuss expectations. When it comes to finances, the best gift is the gift of knowledge. Helping a child become financially aware and financially independent is a lasting display of love.

A weekly meeting for the family is an important step. Each family will have its own guidelines for discussion. Include everyone in the meeting and add the budget as a topic of discussion to help build a strong financial family. If you need to cut back on cable television, discussing the situation beforehand will help temper the shock when that change is implemented.

Some parents feel vulnerable when they speak openly about their finances with their children. If you are uncomfortable talking about specifics with your children, you can speak in generalities. Children also benefit from reading books about finances, such as *Junior's Adventures* by Dave Ramsey[12] or *Play the Real-Life Money Game with Your Teen* by Sarah Williamson.[13] The process of including kids and providing resources helps create financial remapping for future generations.

If you are single, you should still set a weekly appointment for yourself to evaluate your budget. There are numerous little things people say they cannot live without, and with a little ingenuity, you will find there are several ways to modify your finances.

---

12   Dave Ramsey, *Junior's Adventures* (Brentwood: Lampo Press), 2003.

13   Sarah Williamson, *Play the Real-Life Money Game with Your Teen*, Medina, WA: The Real Life Money Game, LLC, 2006.

Make a Conscious Choice

Once you learn to work with a list of financial goals and stop operating out of fear regarding money, you will see your efforts transfer to other aspects of your life. You may feel more financially confident once you have a clear vision of where you are and where you want to be.

Empowering yourself financially allows you to care for others rather than being the one who requests care. When you tap into your own financial power, you no longer wait for luck to happen or hope that you win the lottery—you actively take charge of your life.

Understanding this financial process and dealing with your Money Nerve will lay the foundation for a healthier financial future. You are learning to deal with your finances and identify your priorities. You have been given tools to communicate with your financial partners, and now you are ready to make conscious choices.

Your goal is to move forward as who you truly are. Live the life that you choose to live. To me, living a life without restraints and self-judgment—and living it with gratitude—is what makes everything worthwhile.

Call to Action

Cultivate Partnerships

Answer the following questions in your Money Nerve daily journal.

1. Write down your plan to cultivate your support network. Think of ways to encourage yourself to maintain your new financial path and reinforce what you've learned. See how you can get other people on board to hold each other accountable (for example, your financial support group, business partner, life partner, or children).

2. Take some time to assess your financial partners:

   List the people who have the most financial impact on your life.

   Identify each person's Money Nerve.

3. Have a conversation with your financial partners. A constructive dialogue geared toward money problems often results in one person feeling like the bad guy. Write down a discussion starter that is appropriate to your situation. Here are a few ways to begin a discussion about finances from a neutral place:

   "We both know that we are struggling with our financial obligations. I don't see us addressing them together. Would you be open to forming a team so that we can work together and be more effective?"

   "If I were to set up a plan that put you on a budget, would that help you?"

"I feel sabotaged in this financial relationship, and I need to figure out a positive way to resolve it. Are you on board with the idea of starting to put money away? Is that something you would be willing to work toward?"

4. If you have kids, give them some Monopoly money for a week and tell them you will replace the fake money with actual dollar bills at the end of the week. Each day, collect rent money, gas money, insurance money, food money, and utilities money, for instance. This will help them learn which expenses they will need to be aware of when they are on their own. Encourage them to find ways to earn money through doing chores or saving money—perhaps by cutting coupons, carpooling, or eating out less.

Afterword

So here we are. You wanted to change your relationship with money at the start of this book. And now you are changing that relationship. You have brought it to consciousness; you are ready to launch.

This is a long-term relationship that goes on for the rest of your life.

Honor it.
Respect it.
Take it seriously.

Your money relationship never ends, it only changes form. This is one relationship you can't get out of. It's your unique relationship, so how you choose to respond to finances depends on you.

Will you actively participate?
Will you shut down?
Will you plan ahead?
Will you make mistakes?
Will you get back on track when you do?

You control this financial relationship.

Own that.
Take responsibility.

This is your life.
Keep your financial reality in your consciousness.
Talk about money issues with others to help bring them to consciousness, to help them heal.

Set goals.
Make budgets.
Teach financial responsibility to children for future generations.

Forgive yourself for your wants, needs, mistakes, ambition, shame, and guilt. Heal your Money Nerve.

Embrace your financial relationship—
for what it was …
what it is …
and what it will be.

You deserve a healthy relationship with money.
You have earned it—literally.

Are you ready to receive it?

It's your choice.

About the Author

BOB WHEELER IS A CPA WITH OVER twenty-five years of experience. His world travels lead him to diverse points on the globe, especially those at high altitude. He has climbed Mt. Kilimanjaro in Africa, arrived at Everest Base Camp in Nepal, and climbed several smaller mountains in between. With warmth and humor, what he experiences on the road, in the office, or in a Greek marathon feed his wit as a stand-up comic.

Bob grew up in Clarksville, Tennessee, and he graduated from Rhodes College. He now lives in Santa Monica, California where he owns an accounting firm and serves as the CFO of The Comedy Store.

References

Barrett, Tom. "A Healthier Routine." 2002: n. page. Accessed October 4, 2012. http://www.interluderetreat.com/meditate/7things.htm.

Greenberg, Melanie, PhD. "Is Money the Secret to Happiness?" *Psychologytoday.com*. The Mindful Self-Express, Sept. 2012. Accessed October 3, 2012. http://www.psychologytoday.com/blog/the-mindful-self-express/201209/is-money-the-secret-happiness.

Halvorson, Heidi G. "Why More Money Probably Won't Make You Happy." *Positivelypositive.com*. Living, 9 Mar. 2012. Accessed October 3, 2012. http://www.positivelypositive.com/2012/03/09/money-happy/.

Hill, Napoleon. *Think and Grow Rich*. Lexington, KY: Soho Books, 2010.

"Janitor / Stock Expert Leaves Money to School." *The Lawrence Daily Journal-World*, April 19, 1988. Lawrence, Kansas. Vol. 130, No. 110, p.1.

Matthews, Gail M. "Impostor Phenomenon: Attributions for Success and Failure." Paper presented at the American Psychological Association, Toronto, 1984.

"Mental Map." *A Dictionary of Geography.* Second ed. New York: Oxford University Press, 1997. 277. Print.

Pinker, Susan. *The Sexual Paradox: Men, Women, and the Real Gender Gap.* New York: Scribner, 2008. 188.

Ramsey, Dave. *Junior's Adventures.* Brentwood, TN: Lampo Press, 2003.

Telander, Rick. "Senseless," *Sports Illustrated,* May 14, 1990.

Tolle, Eckhart. *The Power of Now: A Guide to Spiritual Enlightenment.* Novato, CA: New World Library, 1999. Print.

Tyson, Eric. *Investing for Dummies.* 5th ed. Hoboken, NJ: Wiley Publishing, Inc., 2008.

Williamson, Sarah. *Play the Real-Life Money Game with Your Teen.* Medina, WA: The Real Life Money Game, LLC, 2006.